Richard Lowry

MOVED BY STEAM

MOVED BY STEAM

Beside the tracks and on the trains, 1962-67

Richard Inwood & Mike Smith

Foreword by
David St John Thomas

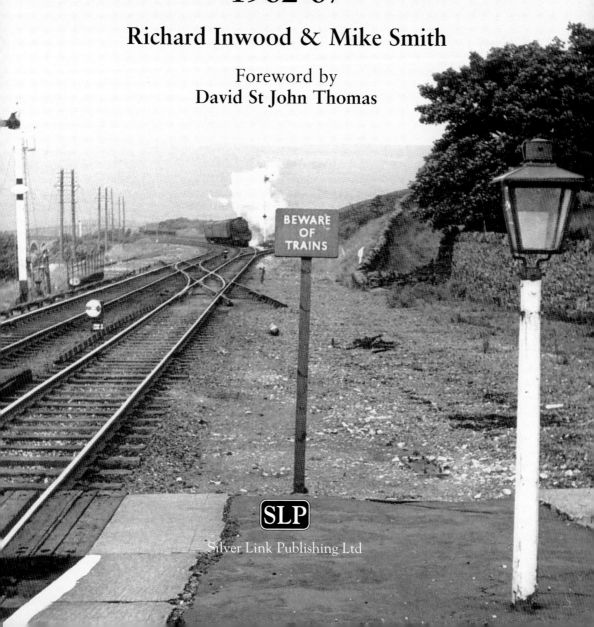

SLP

Silver Link Publishing Ltd

First published in 2009

British Library Cataloguing in Publication Data

A catalogue record for this book is available from the British Library.

ISBN 978 1 85794 323 8

Silver Link Publishing Ltd
The Trundle
Ringstead Road
Great Addington
Kettering
Northants NN14 4BW

Tel/Fax: 01536 330588
email: sales@nostalgiacollection.com
Website: www.nostalgiacollection.com

Printed and bound in the Czech Republic

Richard in the cab of the current Truman's loco, Peckett 0-4-0ST 2136 of 1953, on 24 October 1963. By the time we worked for the brewery in the summer of 1966 (see Chapter 4), shunting was carried out by a road tractor, most of the yard having been concreted. *MES*

Front cover On Saturday 22 May 1965 the 10.45am Bournemouth-York leaves Oxford behind a now unidentifiable 'Hall'. Tantalisingly, Richard's diary entry reads, 'Went with Andrew [Dow] and his friend Robert Wade to Banbury ... had good run, photos, etc.' The red head belongs to the said Robert Wade. *RNI*

Half title Caught in the act! Richard (left) and Mike trespassing in pursuit of steam. Kitson 'dock tank' No 47000 is deputising for an 0-4-0 diesel shunter at James Street Junction, Burton-on-Trent, on 25 June 1964 (see Chapter 4). *Authors' collection*

Page 2 Having been moved by steam from Skipton, we are moved in the other sense by the plumes of steam that greet us at Carlisle. 'Jubilee' No 45697 *Achilles* on the 21.05 FO St Pancras-Glasgow waits for the road into Citadel Station as a 'Black Five' with self-weighing tender takes the Shap line with an early-morning parcels on 24 July 1965. *MES*

Title page At the north end of Garsdale station, a warning to all railways enthusiasts, their families and friends. 'Black Five' No 45254 approaches with the 16.37 Carlisle-Bradford stopper on 24 July 1965. *MES*

Back cover 'Jinty' No 47464 propels its train towards Allsopp's Maltings, Burton-on-Trent, on 25 June 1964. Mike, up the signal post, is securing the elevated view revealed on page 58. A friend appears to be holding the ladder steady. At least the train was moving away from Richard, but such escapades would of course be impossible on today's high-speed, ultra-safety-conscious railway. Trespassing isn't what it used to be! *RNI*

CONTENTS

To Jessica Smith
and in memory of
Cib and Sylvia Inwood and Eric Smith

Above LMS (Ivatt) 2-6-2T No 41249 arrives at Wrafton with an evening local from Barnstaple on 18 August 1964 (see Chapter 7). Mike's mother looks both resigned and anxious: she's used to this sort of thing, but will they catch it? They'll catch it if they don't... *MES*

Left Richard's father (with sunlit cranium) admires 'Royal Scot' No 46152 *The King's Dragoon Guardsman* at Liverpool Lime Street in about 1959. The loco so numbered was really the doyen of the class, No (4)6100 *Royal Scot*; identities were swapped in 1933 for a tour of the USA, and so they remained, though little of either would have been left after rebuilding and the normal processes of replacement. *RNI*

FOREWORD
BY DAVID ST JOHN THOMAS

Here is a book with that tingle factor to bring memories flooding back to those old enough to remember the colourful last days of steam. If you're too young to enjoy that, bad luck, but you'll still gain much from seeing just what you missed and why so much steam survives as part of today's burgeoning tourist industry.

Though they would not claim to be quite in the same league as Eric Treacy, that most celebrated of railway photographers, Richard Inwood and Mike Smith, the authors, were anyway too young to exploit the universal, matter-of-fact steam of Treacy's day. However, even the last days produced fantastic imagery, so well recorded by them in colour and black-and-white pictures, and in their extensive text, which brings to life some of the excitement tinged with sadness of those times.

Mention of Treacy, the famous Bishop enthusiast-cum-photographer, is not accidental. A coincidence: he and Richard, now Bishop of Bedford, were each once Archdeacon of Halifax. What is it about railways and the clergy, even Bishops? The time was when you would go to the local vicar or rector not merely for spiritual advice but because frequently he was the only person in the parish possessing a Bradshaw, whose mysterious innards he would be all too happy to consult. Alas, Bradshaw, Treacy, ordinary working steam … they are all in the past. Our thanks go to the Bishop of Bedford and Mike Smith for, as it were, extending their lease of life. Revel in looking and reading.

Hallowed ground: Carlisle Citadel station was immortalised by Eric Treacy, and it's with some diffidence that we publish pictures taken there. The south end pilot, Ivatt tank No 41222, and a TPO van catch the early morning light on 27 August 1965. *MES*

Peckett 2112 of 1949, the saddle tank at Staton's, Tutbury, en route from the station sidings to the plaster works on 26 June 1965. It once belonged to Truman's brewery in Burton (see page 5 and Chapter 4). Our trusty bicycles star in Chapter 6. *MES*

PROLOGUE

MIKE: As an older colleague used to say, 'numbers come first'; our collections started in 1958. Most of our school-friends were equally fanatical, and the conversation round the first-form dinner-table might go like this. ('Mick' is what Mike, like most Michaels, was called then; 'Phil' is now a distinguished railway photographer; Richard, as a lordly second-former, does not appear.)

Mick	Guess what I copped last night!
Biffo	Summat common.
Mick	Tobago on the Cadbury's.
Phil	You never copped that wreck!
Mick	It's not a wreck, it's rare! It's off Newton Heath!
Steve	Ey Phil, how many Scots do you need?
Phil	Six.
Mick	What's sixty-one-o-eight?
Phil	Seaforth Highlander [you ignorant twit]…

The Burton-on-Trent Grammar School Locospotters' Club met after school in the Woodwork Room. The Woodwork master, Dai 'Taffy' Davies, TD, who also taught Religious Knowledge, was small, Welsh, dignified, and eloquent, and his signature on a request for shed permits lent a spurious respectability to our outings to Crewe or Wolverhampton: spurious because he didn't accompany us (schoolboy rumour, ever unreliable, had it that he was on a canal-boat, drinking pink gins for breakfast), and a fifth-form boy was usually in charge. In these days, when you can't take a school party down the street without

Fun and games with 'A3' No 60048 *Doncaster* at New England depot, Peterborough, in the days before the Health & Safety Executive got out of hand. *RNI*

9

On a "Wanderers" Railfans' Club outing in 1962 one of the highlights was the March stationary boiler, 'J17' 0-6-0 No 65541. A few months later, according to *Modern Railways*, it 'blew all its tubes out … and was removed for scrap.' Note the spotter's Burton Grammar School scarf. *RNI*

completing a risk assessment, it's hard to imagine thirty eleven-and-twelve-year-olds, overseen by a fifteen-year-old, jostling each other on a half-mile walk along the canal bank, or peering through the smoke and picking their way between hot ash-heaps, water-filled inspection pits and moving engines on Stafford Road or Oxley depots. But it was very exciting, and nobody seemed to get hurt. (It was perhaps as well, though, that we weren't around when No 65541 did its little trick at March – see above.)

It's exactly fifty years since Richard and I first met on a railway trip. On 18 August 1959, accompanied by my father, I caught the 7.33am to Sheffield and, on the train, met Richard, who was also having a railway trip north. It was the first of countless excursions we shared over the next seven or eight years.

The older colleague mentioned above, Mike Thompson (another 'Mick' in those days), ran the "Wanderers" Railfans' Club (note the careful punctuation), a more sophisticated society than the Grammar School outfit, with proper coach trips – usually on Sundays, when of course the sheds were full. For a long time my Methodist parents didn't allow me to go on these, and *Lady Patricia* and *Duchess of Montrose*, at Crewe Works on a WRC visit in 1959, never did get into my collection. Oh, the heartache! I've just about forgiven the parents now, but can't help thinking it strange that Richard, who was allowed to go, is the one who's become a Bishop. He was not, however, present on that particular Crewe Works trip, as *Duchess of Montrose* eluded him for ever, as well. Ironically, he owns an OO scale model of her.

Eventually they relented, to the extent of one Sunday outing per year, and the thrill of the Leeds trip on 22 May 1960 is wholly undimmed: Ardsley and Wakefield, crammed with locos, *Royal Engineer* (missed at Burton in 1958) on Holbeck… We got to Mexborough

Above 2 January 1962: we braved the weather for a trip to Swindon Works and the GWR and MR sheds at Gloucester. At the latter, Barnwood, we found 2P 4-4-0s Nos 40540 and 40537, built by the railway that built the shed and now withdrawn. In Ben Ashworth's *The Last Days of Steam in Gloucestershire* there is a similar picture, taken nine days before, without the snow but with No 40540 wearing a 'Waverley' headboard. We didn't remove it – honest! *RNI*

Below On that same wintry January day Pannier tank No 3739 waits to leave Swindon with a westbound local. *RNI*

Above The Great South Wales Expedition of August 1962: No 7826 *Longworth Manor* was a rare bird indeed for us Midlanders. A visit to its nest in Carmarthen on 30 August found it at home and apparently reluctant to leave. *RNI*

Below On the same holiday we found 0-6-0ST No 1365, by then one of the oldest Great Western survivors, still working at St Philip's Marsh, Bristol, on 31 August 1962. Also visible are a 'Grange', possibly No 6846 *Ruckley Grange*, and a 'Castle'. *RNI*

From St Philip's Marsh we walked to Barrow Road depot, then ran to Stapleton Road station, whence a 'Hall' took us to Bath. Here S&D 2-8-0 No 53808 is shunting the Green Park coal stage. *RNI*

in the late afternoon; the first engines were being prepared for Monday duty, and their fires were just being lit. It was hard enough at the best of times to read the number on one of these filthy objects, almost impossible through a foot of pure sulphur. As we strained our eyes, we were surprised to discern a name on the splasher of one of the numerous 'O4s'; unknown to Ian Allan's lists, and traced with a finger in the grime, it read *Sir Archie Ballbag*. Was he the foreman, or the shedmaster?

We were fifteen and fourteen respectively when Mike T. departed to Teacher Training College and we took over the running of the WRC. On coach trips we took a token adult (thank you, Mr Brookes), but the operators were surprised, and probably dismayed, when it was we who gave them directions, got everyone on and off the coach, and handed round the sick-bags. We also took the money and paid the bills, thanks to a cheque signed by Richard's father. It was good fun, and it probably taught us nearly as much about geography, organisation, responsibility and leadership as a Duke of Edinburgh Award would have done.

To start with, photography was only an adjunct to number-taking; we mostly took shed shots, especially of classes small in number or rare to us, to match those in the Ian Allan books. But to the obligatory 'Combine' and 'Shed-book' was soon added the monthly *Trains Illustrated*, and the wonderful pictures of W. J. V. Anderson, Ivo Peters, M. J. Esau, B. J. Ashworth and many others, not to mention Richard's distinguished predecessor Bishop Eric Treacy, inspired us to expand our horizons. (What a nerve we had! Now, when we compare our efforts with theirs, we feel rather as Sir Edward Elgar did when he thought about Beethoven's Fifth: 'Like a tinker may do when surveying the Forth Bridge.') And with the diesels multiplying and the system shrinking, the need to record what we saw became more urgent. Box Brownie 127s were more or less useless for moving subjects, so we petitioned for 35mm cameras as presents at Christmas 1962. To quote J. R. R. Tolkien (another enthusiasm at the time), 'at this point this history begins'.

Above Carmarthen, 29 August 1962. Two 'Castles', the leading one No 5027 *Farleigh Castle*, are ready to take a Paddington express to Swansea. We travelled behind them and they gave us an exciting run. *RNI*

Below After our visit to Bath Green Park on 31 August 1962 we caught the 'Pines Express' to Bournemouth behind a 9F, piloted to Evercreech Junction by a Standard Class 5. Two weeks later this historic train ceased to run via the Somerset & Dorset route. *RNI*

1
CLARITY BEGINS AT HOME
(OR: A SHAKY START)

RICHARD: The hard winter of 1962-63 should have been a good time to begin photography in earnest. Not only were there lots of pretty snow-scenes, but the new diesels (which had taken over all expresses through Burton, Summer Saturdays excepted, in June 1961) didn't like the cold, and steam was summoned to substitute. A report in *Modern Railways* for March 1963 warmed the hearts, though not the fingers, of British steam photographers:

It is obvious that a duty was laid upon the Regions to reduce their steam locomotive stock drastically before the transition from the BTC regime to that of the new BR Board on January 1... It was somewhat ironic that the purge of express passenger steam power in recent months should be quickly followed by the recent appalling weather conditions of January, which seem to have wrought havoc with diesel availability. The state of the Type 4s on the Midland main line was already arousing concern, but by the end of January the availability of these units was reported to have dropped below 50 per cent, through a combination of causes ranging from frost damage to mechanical defects and train-heating boiler failures.

So began the reign of the accountants over railways in Britain; today, when their grip is even tighter, failed trains are simply cancelled.

If the weather was harder in those days, life was harder too. Funds were short, for our parents as well as for us (Mike's never owned a car). No part-time jobs for us, either; we took it for granted that schoolwork (for A levels, by this stage) came first. So we couldn't take full advantage of the photogenic weather. Days out were few, and most of our railway activity was centred on not so very scenic Burton. But this scarcely mattered: at home or away, our pictures were not quite what we'd hoped for. A trip to Worcester on 4 January 1963 (with steam haulage both ways) produced 'Castles' on the Paddington trains and a fine selection of other GW and LMS steam, but not a single shot worth saving, and the same could be said of most of our local efforts, too. Yes, we made all the beginner's mistakes: 1/50sec didn't *quite* stop No 44775 (see overleaf), and if the speed was right the exposure was wrong, and if that was OK we hadn't got the whole train in frame – not to mention the poles in the wrong places. In short, we failed to realise that, however important the subject, the composition is more so. Inspecting some 4,500 images for this book has certainly taught us that lesson – forty years too late!

So stationary portraits still tended to look nicer, and where better to take them than Burton shed? By January 1963, 17B (as we would always know it – 16F from September that year) had lost all its passenger workings. Ironically, it acquired from November 1961 a large cohort of former passenger engines – 'Jubilees', downgraded from such work at Kentish Town, Nottingham, Derby and

Above 'Black Five' No 44775, almost certainly replacing a failed Type 4 diesel, sets out from Burton with a southbound express on 19 January 1963. A northbound freight hides the exit from the shed yard, while the signal gantries in the distance are at Leicester Junction. The vertical stripes on the open wagon indicate that it was a shock-absorbing vehicle; this would have made it suitable for carrying Burton beer, but there seems to have been no consistent effort to match the two. *RNI*

Below Burton shed, January 1963. Local 'Jubilee' No 45667 *Jellicoe* looks too smart to have been taken out of store, but it was certainly transferred to Derby for passenger duties later that month. Also on view are a Stanier 8F and a 9F. Notice the brazier by the water column, and the smoke blown by a north-east wind. *RNI*

elsewhere. These were former star performers on the Midland main line out of St Pancras; we had known them on great expresses like 'The Palatine' and 'The Waverley', and it was sad to see them hauling trippers tender-first (see page 28), and even sadder to see the weaker of them in the shed yard with sacks over their chimneys, like the Reidinger 'Crabs' they were meant to replace. But the same *Modern Railways* article continues:

> The operating authorities were driven to extracting 'Jubilee' 4-6-0s in indifferent condition from store at Burton in order to maintain their services.

Good for the 'Jubes'! Most of those extracted were sent to Derby, but some remained, and more arrived, including Nos 45593 *Kolhapur* and 45721 *Impregnable*, both of which were to regain their former glory on expresses. *Impregnable* achieved great things on an

enthusiasts' special from St Pancras in 1964; transferred to Bank Hall, Liverpool, it worked over Shap in 1965. *Kolhapur* spent three summers operating from Leeds Holbeck over Ais Gill before passing into preservation.

In 1963 the shed had a substantial allocation of other freight locos. P. B. Hands's *BR Steam Shed Allocations* lists, at mid-year, fifteen 4Fs, eleven 'Black Fives', three 'Jinties', and thirteen 8Fs. The depot also serviced, and occasionally repaired, 'foreigners' from far and near. One compensation for the diesel invasion was that the remaining steam locos took a bigger range of duties and were dispersed more widely across the system. So these were stirring times for photographers, as well as number-takers (yes, we still were). From Moor Street, south-west of the station, a tarmac cycle-way, called by us the Shed Path, led to 17B. Trespassing was part and parcel of the risks we took to get the shots we wanted and I – the future clergyman, but less law-abiding then – made regular journeys along the Shed Path, and recorded a wide variety of types.

As we look along the Shed Path in May 1963, Burton stalwart No 44436 trundles by on the Up Slow. *RNI*

Above Inside the earlier (1870) of the Burton roundhouses in the summer of 1963 is long-term local resident, 8F No 48662, beside a visitor in the shape of Stanier 'Mogul' No 42954. These usually arrived off the North Staffordshire line to Tutbury, and were serviced at the main 17B shed after the closure of the LNWR Horninglow sub-shed in 1960. *RNI*

Below Outside, a native between two aliens: Burton 4F 0-6-0 No 44327 between an Ivatt 4MT 2-6-0 and a 9F 2-10-0. *RNI*

Above Grotesque bedfellows. By 1963 the Midland Railway 3F 0-6-0s were some of the oldest and smallest freight locos in the country. A few were still working from Derby, but these examples at Burton on 28 April were already withdrawn. No 43213, in the distance, dates from 1885; No 43793 of 1906 finds itself next to BR Standard 'Britannia' 'Pacific' No 70001 *Lord Hurcomb*, one of the newest (1951) and largest express passenger types. *RNI*

Below Sent to Burton for attention, a most unusual patient on 14 June 1964 is LNER-designed 'J94' 0-6-0ST No 68068. Several of the class were allocated to Rowsley for use on the famous Cromford & High Peak Railway, which we were soon to visit (see Chapters 2 and 7). Note the pleasing fenestration of the 1870 roundhouse. *RNI*

19

Former Crosti-boilered 9F No 92028 has not been sent to the breaker's – it is passing Jackson's scrapyard as it moves tender-first along the Leicester line towards Leicester Junction, probably after turning on the Branston triangle, on 28 April 1963. A surviving MR lower-quadrant signal can be seen beyond. *RNI*

An LNER 'O4' heads the opposite way along the Leicester line in January 1963 with a coal train, perhaps for Drakelow Power Station, whose towers and chimneys can be dimly discerned through the mist. This surprisingly well-loved local landmark was demolished in 2006. *RNI*

We persevered with action shots, too, and the area around the shed was a good place for them. Anglesey Road 'Rec', where Mike failed dismally at Junior School football, gave good views of the shed and the main line. You approached it by a low bridge under the Leicester branch, passing Scrappy Jackson's rotting heaps of metal on the way. This was the route by which railwaymen from that end of town reached the shed, and in our younger days we caused much annoyance to train-crews and to the signalmen at Leicester Junction by hopping over the stile to put halfpennies on the Down Slow, where long coal-trains pressed them into shiny medallions. Even when the diesels were working normally there was plenty of steam activity on freight, and much light engine movement on and off shed. As well as the classes already mentioned you could see Standard '4s' and '5s', 'Austerities', and LNER

'B1s', 'O1s' and 'O4s'. If you were really lucky, a diesel failure on the North Eastern Region would produce a 'V2', or even on the rare occasion an 'A1' on an express, and the 'V2s', as well as 'B1s', also worked Coventry Cathedral excursions up the Leicester line. This remarkable post-war cathedral, with its phoenix-like connection to its bombed-out predecessor, was – and still is – a huge attraction for visitors (see Chapter 2, page 30).

At Branston, a mile and a half further south-west, the town gave way to the country. Beyond the former A38 trunk road, now the A5121 (more of a lane, really, compared with its modern equivalent) and the closed Branston station, there was a boarded crossing, and shots from here, at rail level, could give an impression of looming power.

However, our main congregating place for many years was across the road from the Shed

Above Once upon a time: Mike at sixteen looks young, innocent and faintly apprehensive as Stanier 2-6-0 No 42978 rumbles over the boarded crossing at Branston with a southbound freight on 1 June 1963. *RNI*

Below Like it used to be: 'Jubilee' No 45685 *Barfleur*, in typical Bristol Barrow Road condition, heads the 8.15am Sheffield-Paignton relief past the former Branston station on Whit Saturday, 1 June 1963. *Barfleur* was a frequent performer in the days when 82E 'Jubilees' worked the fastest expresses through Burton. Most were transferred away on dieselisation; this was one of three to remain until withdrawal in 1964. A few years before we'd have called it a 'wreck' – how we begged its pardon now! *MES*

Perhaps on its way to flatten a halfpenny, as mentioned in the text, 9F No 92081 on the Down Slow passes Leicester Junction and the shed buildings with a steel train in January 1963. *RNI*

A bit further south along the slow line, another 'O4', No 63781, makes for Branston in freezing February fog with another coal train. An 'Austerity' 2-8-0 waits to come off shed. For once, the wrong shutter speed does some good, by enhancing the eerie feeling. *RNI*

Path, just south-west of the station and next to the South signal box, a location known to us as Moor Street Bridge, and to other spotters, apparently, as 'The Gates'. Here a rarely used level crossing served as an escape route for vehicles too tall for the adjacent 9-foot low bridge; quite often tall vehicles risked the bridge anyway, and got stuck. A gruesome rumour concerned an Army lorry that tried it with several soldiers looking over the roof. As a result of these episodes a warning ray was installed, which activated a peculiarly strident hooter. Apart from the occasional entertainment announced by the hooter, there was the brewery line nearby that ran beneath the main line, with similarly restricted clearance, and the excitement of watching trains start away from the station (see Chapter 2, page 32) or the locos of the non-stop ones opening up again after the restriction round the island platform.

As photography took over, we moved to more commanding locations. To the north of the station, the Iron Bridges, a single footbridge but spanning multiple tracks, gave excellent views in all directions (see pages 26-28). This was where Mike started his Burton spotting, where his love affair with the 'Jubilees' began. The names still chime out from one afternoon in 1958: *Hardy, Bengal, Bhopal, Trafalgar, Leander* (the first piloted by a Compound)... And here you were in classic Burton, with a mass of railway material and railway activity: the Victorian station (demolished in 1970) to the south, and a brewery on either side (Ind Coope to the left, Truman's to the right). Their industrial locomotives could sometimes be seen, together with those of Bass (see Chapter 4, pages 54-55). Looking north, past Trent Cold Storage, the Horninglow branch (see Chapter 4, page 57) curved away to the left, and beyond were Little

Above Where we saw most of it: the view towards Burton Station from Moor Street Bridge on 20 June 1964. 'Austerity' No 90345 heads south on the main line, beneath the distinctively truncated LMS starting signal. Burton Station South box and milepost 11 (from Derby) dominate the scene on the left; to the right, graffitied even then, is one of the massive posts of the level-crossing gates. Also visible are the gable-end of the fine 1883 station building, demolished in 1970, and the bay platform used by branch trains to Leicester and Wolverhampton, to be withdrawn in September 1964 and January 1965 respectively. *RNI*

Right Oops! Despite the warning stripes and a 'foghorn' hooter, this incident on 7 April 1964 was one of many at Moor Street Bridge with its 9-foot clearance. *Authors' collection*

The 4Fs were still very active in early 1963. In this view from the Shed Path, No 44247 works hard on the rise from the station. *RNI*

Burton Bridge (then the A50, now the A511) and Horninglow Bridge Sidings. North again took us to Wetmore, where roadbridges and footbridges gave further vantage-points, and the main line was crossed by what we called 'the GN Bank' – actually the North Staffs branch from Horninglow to Tutbury and Crewe, but also used by traffic on the Great Northern branch from Hawkins Lane to Derby Friargate (see Chapter 5). Plenty here, too, to see and enjoy!

Another bridge, Woolley's, gave a different perspective, with the characteristic outlines of the English Grains factory and the Clay Mills Pumping Station (now a working steam museum) in the northward view, and Burton spread out on the southern skyline. This was the edge of the town, and though the famous newt-pond by the bridge had been filled in, the hedges in the lane were a great place for greenfinches' nests, and turtle doves raided the spent grain in the factory yard.

Further north still, at Clay Mills, you were back at rail level, but a boarded crossing beside the little Mill Fleam gave a chance for classic three-quarter shots from a slight elevation. And you were really in the country: this was where Mike went for the earliest coltsfoot flowers, and to see great crested grebes on the worked-out gravel pits.

Right The view north from Woolley's Bridge: on 23 August 1963 the English Grains factory provides a backdrop for Hughes-Fowler 'Crab' 2-6-0 No 42923 on the Down Slow. The 6C shedplate shows that this was a rare visitor from Birkenhead depot, famous as the home of the last 'Crabs', withdrawn in 1967. *RNI*

Below right Looking south from Woolley's Bridge towards Wetmore, brewery chimneys can be seen in the distance, and on the right Oaks (or Spalding's) Wood, below which Richard lived. Saltley 'Jubilee' No 45653 *Barham* heads the 8.40am Bristol-Sheffield on the same day. *MES*

Below The other southward view from Woolley's Bridge, in the 1963 January snow, with an LMS 2-6-4T on a northbound local, either a diesel substitute or the frequently steam-worked 1.00pm SO from Birmingham. Oh, that north-east wind! Across the tracks, the gantries belong to the Burton Constructional Engineering Company, for which Mike's father worked. The distinctive building in the distance is the former town electricity works. *MES*

It might have been 1958: 'Jubilees' on Summer Saturday trains, seen from the Iron Bridges, north of Burton station, amid a plethora of breweriana. No 45610 *Ghana* (*opposite above*) lays a smokescreen as it slows for the station with the 7.30am Newcastle-Paignton on 22 June 1963. In the cool early morning of 20 June 1964 (*opposite below*) No 45622 *Nyasaland* creates its own cumulus clouds as it leaves with an excursion via the North Staffs line. Finally (*this page*) two shots of No 45601 *British Guiana* storming away from its Burton stop with mis-labelled 1N84, the 2.15pm Bristol-York, also on 20 June 1964. This lovely sunny day was the first Saturday of the Summer service; we had waited eagerly to see how much passenger steam there would be, and, with nine trains, including five 'Jubilees', we were not disappointed. *All MES*

Above It wasn't 1958 after all: then, No 45618 *New Hebrides* was at Kentish Town, working expresses from St Pancras, but by August 1963, when this picture was taken, it was at Burton, heading trippers tender-first. Despite such evidence of decline, the view from the Iron Bridges still shows a busy traditional railway, with Standard '5' No 73137 on a southbound freight passing brewery sidings full of wagons awaiting collection. *MES*

Below A welcome sight at holiday periods was the Catterick Camp-Birmingham, a semi-regular relief train for forces on leave, which often produced an LNER 'V2'. No 60982 has just crossed the River Dove and is passing over the Mill Fleam at Clay Mills on 26 March 1964. *MES*

2
OUTINGS FOR THE MANY, OUTINGS FOR THE FEW

MIKE: After the diesel invasion, one productive source of steam on passenger trains was the excursion – extra traffic for which diesels were rarely available. Favoured destinations were Coventry and London via the Leicester line, which had seen no regular passenger steam for some years. These could appear at any time, but three times a year you could see a kind of train now practically or totally extinct: the Bank Holiday outing. This was not a private charter, but a 'special' provided and promoted by the train operating company itself – then, obviously, British Railways. Up to 1964 Burton saw quite a lot of these, to places like Dudley Zoo and Alton Towers, the two most popular; Buxton, sometimes via the Ashbourne line, stopping at stations like Alsop-en-le-Dale and Parsley Hay, long closed to regular passenger traffic; Skegness, via the Great Northern and Derby Friargate; Kettering (for Wicksteed Park); Blackpool; and North Wales. They were very well patronised, and though everyone knows the arguments for abolishing them – we can't compete with the car; the coaching stock lies idle for the rest of the year – one does wonder, as so often, whether the accountants had got their sums right, or indeed whether they had done them at all.

The Dudley trains used the Wichnor Junction-Lichfield line, and those to Alton Towers the Tutbury line (more precisely, North Stafford Junction-Marston Junction); moreover, many of the latter originated on the Leicester branch. So again there was the bonus of steam

passenger trains on lines they didn't normally use. Accordingly, at Easter, at Whitsun and on August Bank Holiday Monday, it was off to Alrewas, Horninglow, Stretton or Anglesey Road, as well as to familiar main-line locations where applicable. My plan for an itinerary by bicycle on Easter Monday, 30 March 1964, reads as follows:

dep   Burton 8.45
arr   Drakelow Cutting [Leicester line] 9.10
         for 9.11 ex-Gresley
stay for 9.50 ex-Gresley (Buxton)
then to Rolleston for 11.39 [and] 12.7 Alton
         Towers
then to Alrewas for 1.16 [to Dudley]

Richard obviously disagreed, because we actually photographed on the North Staffs line in the morning, then travelled on one of these excursions: to Alton Towers. 'Black Five' No 45267 on a train from Leicester gave us an excellent run in 35 minutes (in those days you would have been pushed to do it in that time by car). The Churnet Valley Line was (and its preserved portion still is) highly scenic, and Alton Towers is one of the best bits. We didn't visit the Towers (I never have, but Richard took out the mortgage necessary for a day there with Liz and their three daughters subsequently). We spent several happy hours photographing the empty stock leaving to be stabled elsewhere and the full trains returning to their points of origin. Some of the shots are OK, but how much better many of them would have been if

Above A pair of 'B1s', No 61049 leading, head up the Leicester line from Burton in June 1963, with an excursion, probably for Coventry. *RNI*

Below Further towards Leicester, 'Black Five' No 45269 prepares to traverse the hilly South Derbyshire/West Leicestershire coalfield as it passes Drakelow with a special in October 1964. The lines on the left led to Drakelow Power Station. *MES*

we'd thought more about the trees, the signal posts, and the castle on the skyline, and less about the motive power!

Then there was what we called the Footex – the football special. As Burton spotters we used to love these: I shall never forget 9 January 1960, when Leeds Holbeck sent out Carlisle Kingmoor 'Jubilee' No 45728 *Defiance* for a Leeds-Aston Villa match. They had declined by 1963 and we have few pictures of them, but an event on 27 April that year saw us, and enthusiasts all over the Midlands, heading for Birmingham with shutters cocked. In the semi-finals of the FA Cup, Southampton was playing Manchester United at Villa Park, and Bulleid 'Pacifics' worked through to Snow Hill. What joy!

Above A prize indeed for the photographer: 4Fs Nos 44439 and 43888 doubling-heading at Branston on their way back to Mansfield after an outing to Dudley Zoo on Whit Sunday, 2 June 1963. *RNI*

Below 'Black Five' No 45144 climbs away from the Trent past Alrewas on Easter Sunday, 29 March 1964, with another Mansfield-Dudley day trip. *RNI*

Above Next day, Easter Monday 1964, sister engine
No 45264 is also having to work hard as it takes the third
way out of the valley, the North Staffordshire line towards
Tutbury. It is passing Stretton Crossing en route from
Wolverhampton to Alton Towers, a journey using three
lines since closed, including this one (see Chapter 5). *MES*

Below With Burton families aboard, 'Jubilee' No 45561
Saskatchewan pulls out of the station past Ind Coope's
Bottling Stores and Moor Street Gates with a Whit
Tuesday excursion on 4 June 1963. *RNI*

Gothic gloom awaits the Easter Monday excursionists who have just disembarked at Alton Towers. The heavy train has arrived from Crewe behind Standard '5' No 73069 and 'Black Five' No 45033. *RNI*

Rush-hour at Alton Towers on 30 March 1964: No 45264 waits its turn to start the journey home to Wolverhampton as No 45088 brings in the stock of a Birmingham train. *RNI*

No 45264 finally gets away. In the background yet another 'Black Five', No 45267, will soon be off to Leicester. Scenes like this would soon be a memory – the line through Alton Towers closed at the end of the year. Did those hundreds of trippers stay at home in 1965? Or go elsewhere? Pretty soon they would all be on the roads. *MES*

Above 'Royal Scot' 4-6-0 No 46115 *Scots Guardsman*, since preserved, has arrived at Birmingham New Street with a special for the Manchester United-Southampton match on 27 April 1963. *MES*

Below Bringing Southampton supporters, 'West Country' 'Pacific' No 34009 *Lyme Regis* arrives at Birmingham Snow Hill on 27 April 1963, piloted by 8F 2-8-0 No 48478. *MES*

RICHARD: The Crankex – the enthusiasts' excursion, usually a charter – is still with us, and in force, so let us be thankful: the RCTS, SLS, Warwickshire Railway Society, Ian Allan and Alan Pegler were the forerunners of Pathfinder, Vintage Trains and Steam Dreams. With hindsight, in 1963 a 'Patriot' from Wolverhampton to Crewe might have been more valuable than a 'Clan', and a 'Crab' over the Leicester line than a Bulleid 'Pacific', but we all liked the novelty, and the parallels with today are amusing!

I went on the 'Clan' tour, but usually we just chased them – literally, in the case of a visit to Burton by a 'Merchant Navy' 'Pacific'. I was learning to drive, and having photographed the loco as it turned on the triangle by Anglesey Road 'Rec', we raced through the town in an effort to 'catch' it with its train at Woolley's Bridge. Fortunately it was a Sunday afternoon, with (in those days) little traffic, so 'Put your foot down,' said my father, and we nearly hit the roof on the level crossing at Horninglow Station. We made it – just! Fewer problems then about trackside access, but there were exceptions! (See the pictures overleaf.)

Even more memorable was an RCTS special to the Cromford & High Peak (for more pictures of this line, see Chapter 7). Nicely turned-out 'B1' No 61360 brought folk to Parsley Hay and picked them up at High Peak Junction; two 'J94s' were used from Parsley Hay to Middleton Top, and single ones from there to Sheep Pasture and from Cromford Wharf to High Peak Junction. Evidently Health & Safety was no more of an issue than in 1962 (see the Prologue), for the lucky punters stood (!) in mineral wagons for the C&HPR stages, though they did have to walk down the inclines!

Above BR Class 2MT 2-6-0 No 78028 takes the Burton-Leicester line past Anglesey Road 'Rec' with an enthusiasts' excursion returning to Market Harborough on 10 April 1965. The engine is nicely turned out, but in the 'economy' unlined livery adopted towards the end of steam. *RNI*

Right This railtour on 24 March 1963 brought a 'Clan' 4-6-2, No 72008 *Clan Macleod*, from Leeds to Tyseley, Wolverhampton and Crewe. It is seen here at Wolverhampton, piloted by 'Modified Hall' 4-6-0 No 7929 *Wyke Hall*. *RNI*

Above Not a bad shot in the circumstances (see the text): SR 'Merchant Navy' No 35003 *Royal Mail* accelerates away from Burton under Woolley's Bridge with a Crankex returning to London on 1 March 1964. *RNI*

Below 'Get back on the ******* station!' The railwayman's indignation is understandable – despite the condition of the track, this was the main line through Platform 1 at Derby. Unrebuilt 'West Country' 'Pacific' No 34006 *Bude* stands in Platform 2, having arrived from London with a cargo of enthusiasts on 11 May 1963. *RNI*

The next four photographs show the RCTS High Peak Rail Tour of 27 June 1964, with standing room only. In the first (*above*) 'J94s' Nos 68079 and 68012 negotiate one of the C&HPR's famous curves, at Longcliffe, and are then seen (*below*) at the ungated crossing near Prestwich Intake Quarry. *Both RNI*

Passenger power takes over for the descent of Middleton Incline (*left*), and (*below*) No 68006 waits at Cromford to convey the weary punters on the final stage to High Peak Junction. *Both RNI*

3
DISTANT DEPOTS:
THE LURE OF THE UNKNOWN

MIKE: In 1963 we had not yet kicked the number-taking habit, so during that summer we organised two major expeditions, one to Southern Region depots and one to Scotland. The older steam types were dying around us (and even some of the newer ones – the first Bulleid 'Pacifics' went in 1963), while the magazines carried long, depressing lists of withdrawals, and photos labelled 'Class Extinct'. Many of these things were quite unknown to us: we'd never been to the Central Division of the Southern, and those 'Hs', 'Ks', 'A1Xs', 'C2Xs', and even the more recent 'Qs' (a sort of thin 4F) were exotic and intriguing.

As for Scotland, I had never been there, and for all spotters any distance south of the border it was the Promised Land. The sight of a Scottish shedplate, including those of Carlisle (Kingmoor), 12A now, but 68A and Scottish until 1957, the large numbers and/or a 'tab-catcher' on the cab side, made you leap into the air, and if it was a 'namer' you lost control altogether. I expect Mike Thompson's ear still has the scar of a jab from my pen when I flung up my arms as No 45673 *Keppel* of 67A Corkerhill (Glasgow) – and lately of the still-more-coveted 63A Perth – thundered through Tutbury with the up 'Ekker', the lunchtime Manchester-St Pancras express, on 1 August 1960. (This was one of the short-lived, but scheduled, re-routed expresses during the electrification of the West Coast Main Line.) And what about all those veterans of the North British and the Caledonian? We'd

only seen their pictures – we wanted to see *them*.

Some of the antiques, both Southern and Scottish, were still working, but many of the withdrawn ones could still be seen too. Taken out of service much faster than they could be scrapped, they stood in corroding lines at Eastleigh, at Hove, at Lugton, at Bo'ness. 'Copping' a withdrawn loco was a bit of a cheat, of course (though if it was one of your last ten 'Jubes', or a 'Schools'...). But at least they could be photographed, for the record and for our personal memory banks.

The Southern trip started with a coach-ride from Birmingham, which used the part of the M1 then opened. (If we could have afforded it, of course, we'd have gone with steam from Nottingham to Marylebone, or Worcester to Paddington.) We visited Norwood Junction, Nine Elms, Stewart's Lane and Feltham, as well as the WR depot at Southall. A good deal of good stuff, but there was a sense of time running out, and just not the same impression of crowded life as we'd had on a London visit in April 1961. Before an overnight stop at the YMCA, we'd arranged to squeeze in a visit to a Prom – Mozart's Symphony No 39, Berlioz's *Harold in Italy*, and was it some concert excerpts from *The Magic Flute*? We didn't quite make the Albert Hall for 7.30; a kind attendant let us in part-way through the first item, but he regretted it when we let a door slam and added our bit to the broadcast...

Left A sad sight indeed: 'Schools' 4-4-0 No 30930 at Redhill MPD on 13 August 1963. The nameplate has gone but the green paint still gleams and the headcode discs are still in place. *Radley* had moved to Brighton from the Eastern Section after electrification; from expresses like the 'Man of Kent' to seasonal and secondary work was a sorry tale of decline for a famous class, and now came the inevitable, far from happy, ending. *RNI*

Below left A well-known duty for the surviving 'Terriers' (LB&SCR 'A1X' 0-6-0Ts) was as shed pilots at Brighton. No 32640 poses for us on 13 August 1963. *MES*

Below Spotters and passengers alike pay proper attention to rebuilt 'West Country' No 34095 *Brentor*, arriving at Salisbury on 14 August 1963 with the 9.00am Waterloo-West of England express. We were off for a day's shed-bashing at Exmouth Junction and Yeovil, but the other travellers are equipped for a night or two away. The luggage (including a fishing-rod), the barrow, the porter and not least the steam engine lend significance to the occasion: this is to be a real journey on a real train. One young man nonchalantly views it all from the peace and quiet of the opposite platform. *RNI*

Above In a photograph taken from the train in the previous picture, we see routine maintenance on the road for pannier tank No 5410 with the Yeovil Town shuttle at Yeovil Junction on 14 August 1963. *RNI*

Below Unrebuilt 'light Pacific' No 34020 *Seaton* tops the bank from Exeter St David's to Central with an express for Waterloo on the same day. *RNI*

Above Spot the loco: two Austin A40 Somersets, an A35 (is it?), a Reliant and a Ford Prefect bring as large a lump to the throat as unrebuilt 'Battle of Britain' No 34055 *Fighter Pilot*, scarcely visible behind the gleaming array of the staff's pride and joy at Eastleigh Works on 15 August 1963. *RNI*

Below The riches of Eastleigh: among a total of eighty-eight locos on shed, vintage 'E6' 0-6-2T No 32417 and 'Q' 0-6-0 No 30548 are two of the types we've come to see on that day. *MES*

Up early next day for Redhill, Brighton, Hove, Three Bridges, Tunbridge Wells and Guildford, we were rewarded by most of our desired classes in steam, including the Brighton 'A1X' shed pilot in that splendid setting under the cliff. There were bonuses, too: a trip in a push-pull set from Three Bridges to Tunbridge Wells behind (or was it in front of?) an 'H', and unexpected power from Guildford to Reading in the form of a 'Q1'.

After a night chez Mike Thompson in Newbury (more long-suffering parents), it was bus to Salisbury, train to Exeter, and visits to Exmouth Junction and Yeovil – but all the wrong way round, to fit the sheds and not the rides, so no journey on the 'Atlantic Coast Express' (we never did get one, either). As Mike T. wrote later, 'What fools we were at times!' But there was some nice GW stuff at Yeovil, and of course Salisbury to Exeter was Salisbury to Exeter, and it was Bulleid 'Pacifics'. The tour ended with a visit to Eastleigh shed and Works, and if the lines of condemned locos were melancholy, at least we saw most of our remaining exotic desiderata. But *why* didn't we find time for the Hayling Island branch, still working and still 'A1X'? Every time we see a shot of the famous bridge we kick ourselves. What fools, indeed!

•

To get us round Scotland we negotiated for those strange things called Circular Tour tickets, handwritten booklets with sheets torn off (or cancelled, was it?) as you went. The first big decision concerned the outward route: Midland or North Western to Carlisle? Eventually we opted for the 'Long Drag' – by night, to leave more daylight time for the sheds. It was my first overnight trip, and that made it exciting in itself – various incidentals made it more so. The 'Peak' on the first stage to Sheffield had a broken windscreen, but kept going (imagine that now!). We changed there on to the St Pancras-Glasgow relief, and even with another 'Peak' the next leg to Leeds was spectacular, with the fiery walls of the steelworks showing to full advantage. This train was famous as a 'Jubilee' turn from Leeds right up to 1967 (see Chapter 9); in the last years it reversed at City station, but in 1963 it used the avoiding line, changing engines at Whitehall Junction.

With us, as well as Mike T., was Bob from Church Broughton, a big lad who scorned a rucksack and carried a heavy suitcase as if it were a paper bag. One of the things in the suitcase was a massive and powerful flash-lamp. From the window of our train he turned it on a loco waiting nearby as we drew to a stand: 'Jubilee' 45639 *Raleigh*, a well-known Holbeck 'wreck'. The crew, dazzled by the beam, looked over dubiously.

'Are you coming on here?' shouted Bob.

Yes they were, and off we went for our first trip on the Settle & Carlisle. Very exciting, but *Raleigh* was evidently not in good health and, despite a lot of noise and Blea Moor Tunnel lit by a trail of rockets, we lost about 20 minutes to Carlisle, where *Raleigh* was removed. We were held up outside while a 'Royal Scot' came in from Shap – perhaps we should have gone that way...

It was still dark when we turned up at Kingmoor depot (wonder what time our permits were for?). There was plenty to see: eighty-seven locos altogether, including an 'A2', three 'A3s', an 'A4', two 'Semis', two 'Clans', a named 'Black Five', and nine 'Jubilees' (but only one of the old classic Kingmoor rarities, No 45696 *Arethusa*), not to mention a Burton 8F! The rest of the day consisted of falling asleep. En route from Dumfries to Kilmarnock we all did, nearly missing our stop, and confirming what my father learned from wartime travel, that it's easy enough if you get your head down. Then I disappeared at Ardrossan station, to be found dead to the world in the toilet. Finally, according to Richard, we took our ease in a waiting room somewhere on pew-style seats painted episcopal cerise – or was this a dream-vision of his future career?

We woke up from time to time to stumble round yet another depot. Not having done our homework, we were surprised to see not only Caledonian but also North British locos on

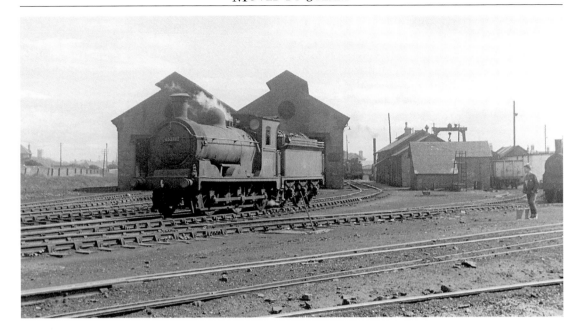

Above North British 'J36' No 65273 0-6-0 was one of a class introduced in 1888. Still working on 24 August 1963, it is framed by the shed buildings in the alien environment of Ardrossan on the 'Sou'-West'. Big Bob, complete with suitcase as described in the text, watches from the right. *RNI*

Left The Caledonian counterpart to the 'J36' was the McIntosh '812' Class, dating from 1899. No 57568 is in steam at Motherwell on 25 August 1963. *MES*

There were only six locos in residence at Kipps shed when we visited on 25 August 1963, but they included a 'J88' (a class introduced in 1904), a 'J83' (1900), a 'Caley Pug' (1885), and this 'Y9' 0-4-0, No 68104 (1882). *RNI*

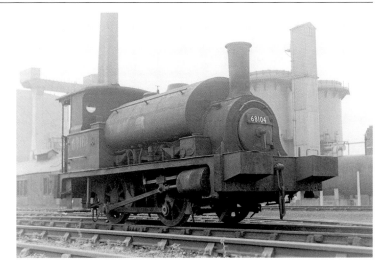

The cabside numbers show that this 'Jubilee' had last been overhauled at St Rollox Works. The big numbers, the small Fowler tender and the single-line-tablet holder were the signs that brought the Sassenach spotter to the heights of ecstasy – here, for sure, was a Scottish 'Jube'. No more trips to England for No 45718, and its next works visit will be to Cowlairs for scrap. It awaits the call at St Rollox shed on 25 August 1963. Nameplates and shedplate have gone: *Dreadnought* of 12A it had been. In two days we'd seen the former *Courageous, Defiance, Furious* and *Perseverance* as well – oh, the irony, the pathos, of those names! *RNI*

Glasgow & South Western territory, and still working. It wasn't until, many years later, I read the books of David L. Smith that I realised things hadn't changed much since 1923: the 'Sou'-West' was still being used as a dumping-ground for types the rest of the system didn't want! We weren't in any condition to take in much else. Ayr depot had No 61007, the 'B1' everyone wanted to see, not only because of its rarity but because it had the most bizarre and intriguing name, *Klipspringer*, in a class that went in for such – but I'd completely forgotten until I look at my notebook now.

A few more memories do stand out from the haze: the incredible fact that the locals really did (and no doubt still do) pronounce 'Troon'

as 'Trin'; the excitement of a number-taker at Kilmarnock over the appearance of a Burton 'Jubilee', No 45622 *Nyasaland*, on the 'Thames-Clyde' relief a week or two earlier (yes, here they got worked up about *English* engines); unlikely station names like Nitshill, Pollokshaws (West) and Crossmyloof (were we still asleep?).

Sunday was the day of the Great Glasgow Shed Bash. We managed to cover eight. We must have traversed some pretty rough areas, and Glasgow had a bad reputation at home (the Gorbals was a synonym for Worst Kind of Slum), but they didn't make much impact. What did impress was the bleakness of the Scottish Sabbath. In search of something to eat,

Above left Chimneys galore: 'J83' No 68477 finds retirement work as a stationary boiler for St Margaret's MPD on 26 August 1963. *RNI*

Left Two sturdy 0-6-0s, Reid 'J37' No 64537 and Gresley 'J38' No 65909, are ready for action at Polmont on the same day. *MES*

Above An appropriate location for 'A1' 'Pacific' No 60152 *Holyrood* at Haymarket, Edinburgh, on 26 August 1963. Another member of the class was *Auld Reekie*: in its absence, No 60152 does its bit for the city's reputation. *MES*

Right On the same day at Haymarket 'A4' No 60024 *Kingfisher* gapes like the bird of its name. *RNI*

we entered the only open shop and made a polite enquiry.

'Ye'll get no fish and chips in Coatbridge today – because *I* don't cuik them,' was the grim reply. Cold Cornish pasties had to do instead.

We saw plenty of steam, from a shedful of 'Caleys', 'WD' 2-10-0s and 'Black Fives' at Motherwell to the famous relics at Kipps; and on Polmadie were those objects of veneration in our earliest days at Lichfield and Tamworth, Nos 46222 *Queen Mary* and 46223 *Princess Alice*. But what spoke to us most strongly and poignantly were the withdrawn LMS passenger locos. Here, at St Rollox and Corkerhill, as at Lugton the day before, were the 'Jubilees' we'd have given the earth to see five years before; and here too were the Scottish 'Scots', rare visitors to the West Coast line south of Crewe and once or twice, amazingly, glimpsed at Burton. Of course, it was nice to see them – some for the first time – but anticlimactic and even a bit embarrassing. A 'dead' loco might be revived; a condemned one was gone for good, scrap metal already. Or so we thought then, in pre-Barry days.

There were more relics in the Edinburgh area. Yes, the 'J36s' with legendary names like *Somme*, *Mons* and *Haig* really did exist, while the now preserved No 65243 *Maude* was even working. But there was also a heartening sense that steam, mainly in the form of 'J37s' and 'J38s', was still earning its keep in the Fife coalfield, and Gresley Pacifics were still alive and well on Haymarket. The townscape of Edinburgh just managed to emerge through the vapour, but the most vivid memory there is a trivial one. A good cheap place to eat in those days was the Steps café at Waverley station. One of my childhood treats had been Heinz spaghetti, and Ham Salad with Spaghetti scored highly when the waitress produced a tin of the latter, opened it at the table, and plonked the entire contents (cold) on the plate. The other Mike was unimpressed: he'd been reluctant to eat at the Steps because on his last visit he'd found a piece of string in, guess what, a ham salad.

'Oh, come on,' we said, 'don't be daft, it's not going to happen again.'

And there, lurking beneath his ham, was … yes, really. Now we think it must have been deliberate, a proclamation that this was good home-cooked Scottish fare. But then – how we larffed!

We had decided to make Perth our northern limit, and there and at Stirling there was plenty for the camera, both on and off shed. We knew, of course, about the 'A4s' on the Glasgow-Aberdeen three-hour trains, but numbers still came first and we allowed ourselves only one unexciting snippet, from Glasgow to Larbert behind No 60031 *Golden Plover*. Bob almost failed to catch this one: as a BR employee, he had a privilege ticket of an even more arcane nature than the Circular Tour, and it certainly mystified the Inspector at Buchanan Street. Finally, this worthy concluded 'Ye're way out of your route, mon!' but let him through all the same, just in time. I, at least, wish our priorities had been different: more miles behind 'A4s' would have been good, and what about those 'A1s' and 'A3s' at Haymarket and St Margaret's?

Edinburgh-Newcastle with a 'Deltic' is OK in retrospect, but surely we could have found some steam? Gateshead was dripping with it (but without a permit we got no further than the office), and Heaton and Blaydon – where an eating place put the Steps in the shade by offering Beef Pie and Chips for 1s 2d – weren't bad. We did manage Newcastle-Darlington behind an 'A3', and were awed by our first sight of Durham Cathedral from the railway. Darlington Works and shed gave us some more sad sights, as well as some smart ex-works ones, then it was off home to arrive on the Bristol mail in the early hours.

I celebrated the end of the trip by closing my number collection (perhaps I was just too lazy to underline all 889 cops in my 'Combine'?). As a grand finale it had its points, but it might have been better had I closed the collection *before* the trip, and spent the time and money on action shots and rides. Imagine if we'd passed the Saturday at Beattock or Waverley instead of Dumfries and Ayr, or spent another night on the train, say along the 'Port Road' to Stranraer on the 'Northern Irishman'…

Above More chimneys: two of the famous Caledonian 0-4-4 passenger tanks, Nos 55204 and 55269, show off their stovepipes at Perth depot on 27 August 1963. *MES*

Below And yet more: Caledonian 'Standard Goods' No 57261 stands by the gasworks at Stirling on the same day. *RNI*

A contrast in profiles (and condition) at Stirling station on 27 August 1963: Gresley 'V2' 2-6-2 No 60955 with the 1.30pm Aberdeen-Glasgow (*above*) and Stanier's rebuild of 'Patriot' 4-6-0 No 45535 *Sir Herbert Walker KCB* on a southbound parcels. *MES/RNI*

Above Moved by smoke: we are homeward bound from Scotland on 28 August 1963, and somewhere up ahead is 'A3' 'Pacific' No 60054 *Prince of Wales*, passing Gateshead West on the 2.35pm Newcastle-York. The unpainted aluminium window frames testify to the newness of the BR Mk 1 coach – they would be painted when it became due for shopping. Nevertheless, the vehicle bears the stamp of history: the second window from the photographer, with its thicker frame, was hinged to allow the passage of stretchers carrying convalescent victims of the Second World War. *MES*

Below A more traditional view of No 60054 with the same train under the fine overall roof at Darlington. *MES*

Above In some parts of the world this 'J39' 0-6-0 might have been forgotten as well as abandoned, and the Gresley fans might have been able to preserve a member of the class. No such luck for No 64886, found in an overgrown corner of Darlington Works on 28 August 1963. *RNI*

Below The 'J27s' did better: several worked in the North East until 1967, and one survives in preservation. No 65814, seen during the same visit, has just been outshopped at Darlington. *RNI*

4
BACK TO BURTON

RICHARD: The lure of the faraway was strong. But really our home area was very rich and, as ever, we could with hindsight have made much more of it. Burton was famous for its brewery railways, and especially for the amazing number of level crossings (counts vary from twenty-seven to more than thirty – as many as thirty-two in 1890, we're told), which disrupted road traffic even on the major streets in the centre of the town. These lines penetrated most of the older areas, finding their way to places unreachable by road or footpath, passing or even entering buildings of great industrial archaeological interest, and they preserved much fascinating ancient railway furniture. Now that they've gone, now that most of the buildings have been demolished and the land redeveloped (which mostly, in Burton, means turned into car-parks), we wish we'd spent more time recording them and the motive power that worked them: the wonderful little saddle-tanks of Bass, Ratcliff & Gretton (turkey red), Worthington (dark blue), Truman, Hanbury & Buxton (dark green), and Marston, Thompson & Evershed (dark blue), even the locally built Baguley diesels (dark green) of Ind Coope & Allsopp, as well as BR machines (black). All credit to the great R. C. Riley and to our Grammar School colleagues Cliff Shepherd and Roger Newman, who did, and to Cliff and to people like Nelson Twells for publishing books about them. Still, we managed a little.

By our time the branch to Marston's brewery (home of the last surviving example of the Burton Union brewing system of giant wooden casks – still extant) was normally diesel-worked, but the reserve was a charming Hawthorn Leslie 0-4-0ST of 1924. My father worked for Marston's, so it was easy to get news of when the diesel was out of action. We failed to take its picture on the bridge that carried the branch over the Trent & Mersey Canal, but I managed to get several of the loco, some in steam, and, later, some sad ones of its removal by road to the Foxfield Railway for preservation.

In the summer of 1966 we both worked at Truman's, earning a bit to take us on a holiday to Spain. The job itself could be challenging, both physically (stacking crates of bottles) and socially (we were very innocent, and our colleagues' evening recreations, and the black-and-white photos they took as evidence, were rather different from ours). But they were kind to us, even when in a subsequent year I managed to ruin a lorry's front bumper while parking a second one! The rail connection there no longer existed, but we had some pictures from earlier years (see page 4).

Some of the industrial lines were worked and/or owned by BR. The Midland Railway Horninglow branch crossed Mike's home street (see Epilogue, page 125), and served a number of more or less run-down industrial premises; it had originally run to a wharf on the canal. Until early in 1961 this branch had been worked by Midland Deeley 'dock tanks', then it passed to 'Jinties'. Another interesting 'Jinty'

Three portraits of Bass's brewery locomotives, taken in the second half of 1963. In the first (*above*), 0-4-0ST No 9 (Neilson Reid 5907 of 1901) is seen at Shobnall, propelling a train including one of the firm's own tank wagons. No 2 (*below*), another Neilson Reid product (5760 of 1900) poses prettily at Allsopp's Crossing. The line from Ind Coope & Allsopp's brewery, which crossed the Midland Railway Guild Street branch here on the flat, can be seen to the left of the loco. Finally (*below right*) No 9 is seen again, waiting to leave the Bass complex at Shobnall. *All RNI*

line served Allsopp's Maltings at Shobnall, almost next to the house where I spent most of my childhood. Like the Marston's line, it had its own bridge over the canal, and was practically inaccessible except by walking the track. The few grain vans went up and down on a weekday morning, when of course we were usually at school. What better use for one of Mike's A-level revision days than chasing it? (I had had a third year in the Sixth Form and was more or less a gentleman of leisure by this time.) We were in luck, too, because the recently closed Dallow Lane branch, from which the Maltings line diverged, was having some attention that day from a permanent way gang. We were able to follow the loco up and photograph it in this by now rare location. The line had also been used for storing wagons; noticing one day that they were moving, Mike ran for the camera and was rewarded by now-preserved 'Black Five' No 45407. Some seven years earlier, at the tender age of eleven, I photographed a rare, if not unique, occurrence on this line. It also featured a 'Black Five', on this occasion No 45091, hauling a passenger train, the RCTS special 'The Mercian' on 2 June 1957 (see page 59).

Mike should have been revising in the evenings, too, but the A-level period happened to coincide with an overhaul period for Burton's only 0-4-0 diesel shunter, No D2859. This was used for the Bond End and New Street branch, some of the curvature of which was really too sharp for a 'Jinty'. The substitute, sent from Derby, was Kitson saddle tank No 47000. We followed this into some very arcane areas of downtown Burton, including a part of the town centre invisible from any street (and now, inevitably, a car-park). The consequence for Mike of neglecting the revision was missing a predicted grade A in Spanish – but how much nicer to have the photos!

There were other small lines and comparable branches elsewhere around Burton, particularly in South Derbyshire, but for good or ill we didn't bother with them – except for one. Staton's plaster mill in Tutbury, now a recreational area, had a rail connection to the North Staffs Derby-Crewe line (see page 8). The tiny system had picturesque buildings and an even more picturesque bridge over the River Dove. A lovely June day in 1965 produced some good footage there.

Even then there was still a fair bit of steam-hauled freight on the main line through Burton, and a few more locations were exploited. But from 1964 attention began to shift to a more scenic route out of town, and the results of time spent there deserve a chapter to themselves.

Left Marston's No 3, Hawthorn Leslie saddle tank 3581 of 1924, outside the brewery in August 1963. The regular diesel was evidently under overhaul or repair. *RNI*

Left Activity inside Marston's brewery, seen through a spectacle glass of No 3, at the time of the same steaming in 1963. *RNI*

Below Marston's No 3 passing Richard's house in Shobnall Road, Burton, en route to the Foxfield Railway on 12 April 1967. *RNI*

Above BR evidently had difficulties serving the Horninglow branch in October 1964. The line was visible from Mike's house, and 4F No 44597's foray was the only visit by a tender engine he ever witnessed. 'NOT FIT TO LOAD' has been chalked on the leading wagon. *MES*

Below A month or two later things were more normal, with faithful 'Jinty' 0-6-0T No 47643 on its accustomed turn. The fireman opens the gates at Victoria Street. *MES*

Above Elderflower time: Allsopp's Maltings, where 'Jinty' No 47464 is shunting grain vans on 25 June 1964, were right on the edge of town, at the end of a branch built in 1880. Oaks Wood, to the right, is now a nature reserve, but the Maltings, with the meadow in the foreground, are long gone. *RNI*

Below No 47464 propels its train towards Allsopp's Maltings. The elevated view was secured by climbing a disused signal post (see the back cover). Bass's and Marston's brewery chimneys are prominent, as is the branch's own bridge over the Trent & Mersey Canal. Who planted the clump of trees beside the bridge (a local landmark), and why? *MES*

Above Also on 25 June 1964, No 47464 runs up the closed Dallow Lane branch by Dallow Bridge to collect a permanent way gang. The canal can be seen above the cab roof. *MES*

Below This is one of first railway photographs Richard took, just before leaving Primary School. On 2 June 1957 'The Mercian' RCTS special approaches Shobnall Road Bridge on the Dallow Lane branch behind 'Black Five' No 45091. The small building on the right housed the borehole of Magee Marshall & Co, whence regular consignments of Burton water were sent to their brewery at Bolton. *RNI*

Above Burton 'Black 5' No 45407, now preserved, and famous *inter alia* for its part in the forty-year-on re-creation of the 1968 'Fifteen Guinea Special', clears wagons from the Dallow Lane branch in January 1964. On the right are the Shakespeare Road flats; nearby lived our late colleague Robert 'Biffo' Smith, as did Nicholas Whittaker, author of *Platform Souls*. MES

Below In June 1964 Derby's Kitson 'dock tank', 0-4-0ST No 47000, stood in for Burton's resident diesel on the tightly curved New Street and Bond End branches. On 25 June, at the former Robinson's brewery behind Station Street, it has penetrated to the very heart of Burton, but few Burtonians will ever have been there until the 1980s, when – like most of central Burton – it became a car-park. MES

Right A day or two earlier, No 47000 waits at Burton New St No 2 crossing, watched by Grammar School boys. We forbear to comment on the possible application of the 'Persil' advert. *RNI*

Right At Clarence Street Maltings on 25 June 1964, a railwayman looks dubiously at the state of the track that No 47000 and its grain van have to traverse. The goat on the oast-house is a landmark, still there in 2009. *RNI*

Below At the end of its turn of duty, No 47000 waits to take the curve from Dale Street to Leicester Junction and the main line. Engine and train seem to blend only too well with the contents of Mr Moore's scrapyard. Moor Street Bridge, with its nine-foot clearance and warning embellishments, can be glimpsed beyond; Burton Station South signal box is to the right. *RNI*

An idyllic scene at Tutbury as the local Peckett saddle tank propels its train over the River Dove towards Staton's plaster works on 26 June 1965. *RNI*

Above Here we are at the works on the same day, with some fine private-owner wagons and some very crude lumps of gypsum. *RNI*

Below At Croxall, beyond Wichnor Junction, the Burton-Birmingham main line crosses the rivers Tame and Trent on a viaduct, continued as an embankment. A 9F heads south with a York (Dringhouses)-Bristol fitted freight in April 1965. *MES*

5

'THE ANNESLEY' AND 'THE COLWICK'

MIKE: The Great Northern Railway's route from Nottingham Victoria to Derby Friargate, Egginton Junction and Burton, with the extension from Uttoxeter to Stafford it purchased in 1880, is the subject of Mark Higginson's splendid *The Friargate Line*. The Burton-Derby section, which closed to ordinary traffic in 1968 (the Egginton Junction-Mickleover section was retained until the 1990s as a research and experiment facility), was much more scenic, as well as much longer, than the Midland line from Burton to Derby. The latter spends half its length in the Trent valley, and runs into housing and industry well before Derby. The Friargate line climbed steeply away from the valley, and the spur from Horninglow, terminus of the trains that feature in this chapter, had another climb right at the start, to a bridge over the Midland at Wetmore. There were excellent photo-points all the way along, though some were rather inaccessible, and even the Derby approaches were more attractive than those of the MR.

There were no regular passenger trains between Burton and Egginton after 1939, apart from the famous Summer Saturday service from King's Norton to Skegness, which lasted until 1964, but in our day it still saw a good deal of freight. Two trains in particular had a large enthusiast following. These were the 6.15pm Horninglow-York (later Sheffield) and the 6.55pm from the same yard to Colwick, east of Nottingham. The second, naturally, was called 'The Colwick' (and usually had a Colwick locomotive), but we called the first 'The Annesley', because Annesley, north of Nottingham, was where the inbound train of its engine originated, that engine itself being sometimes, but by no means always, from Annesley depot. Over the years, in fact, these trains produced a great variety of locos, that being the original source of their popularity. Up to 1962 'The Annesley' was usually a York 'B16' and 'The Colwick' a Colwick 'K3', but 'J39s' and 'K1s' could also appear. How we wished we'd had decent cameras before the elegant 'K3s' became extinct (see Chapter 7, page 80)! From 1963 the commonest classes were 9Fs, 'B1s' and, later, 8Fs, with the occasional 'Black Five', but by then we were starting to care less about the locos and more (though not enough) about the trains, so 4N19 and 5E10 retained their following despite the waning interest of the motive power.

The most popular locations were the climb out of Burton through Stretton & Claymills, the cutting south of Rolleston-on-Dove and the embankment north of it, and some picturesque spots around Etwall, on the Derby side of Egginton. The line between Stretton and Rolleston is now the 'Jinny Trail', a nature trail commemorating the 'Tutbury Jinny' (always so pronounced, but sometimes spelt 'Jenny'), the Burton-Tutbury auto-train withdrawn in 1960, which shared that section of track with the Friargate traffic. The line had plenty of natural history interest in the 1960s, too, and some of our pictures have a feeling of rural tranquillity hard to find in the area today, though it persists in the little-visited (and private) riverside pastures north of Rolleston. These images recall particularly the early summer evenings of the mid-'60s, relaxing bike-rides after tea along quiet roads in evening light, with the smells of cow parsley and hawthorn and mown grass, all somehow symbolic of the 'Sixth Form Years', with – in those days at least – their special balance of security and freedom, and the prospect of more exciting things to come. The end of those halcyon days came for Richard in July 1964, for me a year later, in the month that also saw the end of steam on 'The Annesley' and 'The Colwick'.

Above On 13 July 1963 'Black Five' No 44810 heads the 8.50am King's Norton-Skegness train, which is about to cross Derby Road, Burton, then the A38. The Exeter-Leeds Trunk Road (as it was officially called) had to negotiate five level crossings on its passage through the town, but perhaps the disruption was not so very great: this is 10 o'clock on a summer Saturday morning, and the traffic queue consists of half a dozen vehicles. *RNI*

Right York's ex-LNER 'B16' 4-6-0 No 61448 stands in front of the former Horninglow shed of the LNWR on 18 March 1963, before returning home with the 6.15pm beer train. These handsome engines had been regular power for this train for many years, and this was the last one we saw on it. It looks very smart in the evening sun, but this was also the evening of its life: it was withdrawn in June 1964, together with the other remaining members of the class, and none was preserved. *MES*

Left Horninglow shed again, on
18 June 1965: 'B1' No 61145 waits
to leave with the 18.55 – yes, the
LMR had started to use the 24-hour
clock just four days before! – to
Colwick. Several of the other
buildings, including the water tower,
are still there. *MES*

Below Another 'B1' passes Stretton
Junction with 'The Colwick' in July
1964. Unlike the backdrop of
previous picture, this one has
changed beyond recognition: the
most prominent landmarks, Holy
Trinity Church and Drakelow Power
Station, have gone. *MES*

Right 'The Colwick' again, just past
the site of Stretton & Claymills
Station on 23 June 1965. No 61285
is having to work hard, but the
fireman on this turn will soon have
an easier life – steam gave way to
diesel the following month. *MES*

Below right A little further along the
line, Colwick's own No 61188
approaches Rolleston station
in April 1964. *MES*

Above Hawthorn time, May 1965: the driver of this 'B1' has shut off for Dove Junction, where the train will take the GN spur to Egginton. *MES*

Below No 61188 again, on the GN line north of Etwall in June 1964. The 'unimproved' pasture dates the scene almost as much as the steam loco. *MES*

6
ON YER BIKE

MIKE: Sixth Formers didn't have cars in those days, and parents, however long-suffering, were less willing to lend theirs, even if they had them. The train was expensive. Much of the time it was the push-bike for us.

The West Coast Main Line was only 12 miles or a bit more away at Tamworth, Lichfield, Armitage and points between. If we'd thought harder, or been better advised, we'd have chosen our vantage-points better: the Trent Valley stretch is often level with its surroundings, or slightly embanked, and though 'looming monster' shots have a certain charm we were obviously thinking yet again of the subject rather than the composition. Why didn't we exploit the canal at Whittington, or the historic station at Atherstone, or go that bit

further to Milford, on the fringe of Cannock Chase? Ah well...

Our success was greater with the eastward continuation from Derby of the Friargate line, which still carried passengers up to September 1964. As with its Burton end, described in Chapter 5, the easy route between Derby and Nottingham was occupied by the Midland,

City of Lichfield at Lichfield: No 46250 heads the down 'Lakes Express' (11.40am Euston to Windermere and Workington) on 31 August 1963. 'Semis' was our name for the Stanier 'Pacifics'; they were the highlight of a day out at Lichfield Trent Valley or Tamworth, and this was the last time we saw them there on regular expresses. Mike had a wonderful run behind preserved No 6233 from Euston to Crewe in 2006, and it brought that day in 1963 vividly to mind. *MES*

'Britannia' No 70020 *Mercury* heads the 11.25am Euston-Llandudno past Elmhurst Crossing, between Tamworth and Lichfield, on 11 July 1964. Nice enough, but not quite the same as a 'Semi'... *MES*

and when the Great Northern came along its trains had to negotiate the hilly country around Ilkeston. So here too there were good places for photography. Not far beyond Friargate the line climbed in a shallow cutting on the edge of a wood before it emerged at the closed station of Breadsall. As ever, many shots failed to fulfil their promise for lack of a filter, and the unattractive Ivatt 4MT 2-6-0s (we knew them as 'Pigs') that worked the passengers trains were made still less appealing by the absence of a turntable at Derby, which meant tender-first working in one direction. But it was a nice quiet spot to spend the day, and there was plenty to see – not only what we were photographing, but also the Sheffield-Derby line down in the Derwent valley, where on one occasion we saw an 'A1' 'Pacific' substituting for a 'Peak'. 'The fastest thing through Chesterfield for a long time,' we were told.

In 1964 I acquired a new and slightly lighter bike (a Sun Mist) and this made longer journeys easier. Two expeditions stand out from that busy summer: one on a Saturday to the Great Central, still almost entirely steam and still featuring the famous Annesley-Woodford 'Windcutters', and one to the Stafford-Wellington line, which was to close at the end of the season.

Both journeys were a bit of a slog (30-plus miles each way), with some dubious short-cuts – did those white roads on the map, at Ticknall, Tixall, Ingestre, really go anywhere? We remembered the day years before when a track at Haunton, on our most direct route to Tamworth, landed us at a ford quite unfordable by us on the River Mease: calm water in warm sunshine, a rural idyll, but not much help when a summer Saturday on the WCML was still 5 miles away!

All went well in 1964, however, and we reached the summit of the GC north of Loughborough to find an excellent location – locos working hard going south, and bursting from the tunnel going north. No LNER types any more, alas – oh, that all-powerful LMS oligarchy! – but a good variety of other things, including one of Annesley's mostly run-down 'Royal Scots', a GW 'Hall' (on a regular turn), and of course the 9Fs on the 'Windcutters'.

The long haul to Derrington, 3 miles the other side of Stafford, landed us at a Trent Valley-style stretch of track with no good

Above On 13 April 1964 the condition of 8F No 48141 matches the bright spring morning as it climbs away from the Derwent Valley towards Breadsall with a northbound freight on the GN Friargate line. *MES*

Right Coasting downhill towards Derby on the same day, Standard Class 5 No 73010 passes the crossing and signal box at Breadsall Station, closed in 1953. *RNI*

Right Almost invariable power for Friargate line passenger trains in their final years was a 'Pig' – an Ivatt LMS 2-6-0 (what would the Great Northern's directors have said?). No 43108 is in typically grimy condition at West Hallam in January 1964. *MES*

Above An Annesley-Woodford 'Windcutter' behind the regulation 9F climbs to the short tunnel at Barnston summit on the GC line north of Loughborough on 4 July 1964. *RNI*

Below One reason for a long bike-ride from Burton to the GC was the Annesley 'Royal Scots'. No 46122 *Royal Ulster Rifleman* heads downhill towards East Leake with the 2.38pm Marylebone-Nottingham on the same day.

A sad come-down, though, both for the 'Scots' and for the Great Central. The carriage roof-boards seem a brave but rather pathetic attempt to maintain the great tradition of the old Manchester expresses; as for the 'Scots', Colin Walker wrote that they were 'obviously cast-offs from the depots which had sent them … as different members of the Class became mechanically exhausted they would be withdrawn and replaced by others … with life left in them.' *MES*

vantage-points. Just a bit further on, there was much better terrain, but we hadn't got the strength! Still, we saw what we'd hoped for, a Fowler tank (and in splendid nick), and the ride home with a following wind was in lovely evening light.

By 1965 we had bigger ideas. I cut short my Burton Grammar School career to join Richard, down from Oxford, on a bike trip to the Somerset & Dorset. I was sorry to leave school, but my last day was a good one, and not only for the obligatory and (by the school rules) illegal trip to the pub at lunchtime. It was my week for reading the lesson in Assembly, and instead of the prescribed passage we had Ecclesiastes xii – '...much study is a weariness of the flesh' – and instead of the set hymn the rugby players' anthem 'Guide me, O thou great Jehovah'.

Next day we set off for the first night's stop at Winchcombe. Seventy miles proved a bit much, and our room at the Bell was above the Public Bar, so not much sleep was had. Saturday was spent on the Stratford-Cheltenham line – not bad, but no GW steam, and pleasant rather than striking views. On Sunday we faced another long ride: over the shoulder of the Cotswolds to Stroud we pedalled, or sometimes walked, then up and over again to Bath, nearly all of it in heavy rain. We sought shelter, and somewhere to eat our

The Fowler 2-6-4 tanks with their parallel lines always looked more 'right' to us than the tapered Stanier and Fairburn varieties. No 42400 of Stafford makes a fine sight doing the kind of job it was built for on the 5.40pm Stafford-Wellington of 28 July 1964. The line closed to passengers six weeks later. *MES*

sandwiches, on Stroud Station. A strenuous morning, and a pint of cider on an empty stomach, had made us feel rather peculiar. What was an LMS 4F doing there? And was it really propelling its train down the up line? Yes it was (and the fact that it was a breakdown train might have had something to do with it), but there really *was* something wrong with our brains, or mine at least, for my notebook also says '63XX Banking duty' – unlikely, as the last one had been withdrawn the year before. More probably what I saw and photographed was the 'Manor' listed next and seen in the following shot. Oh dear!

We got to Bath soaked and exhausted. A kind elderly landlady dried our outer garments in the oven, but they were soon damp again, for Monday was almost as bad. Those special West Country clouds, like wet grey cotton wool, rolled over, looking too full and heavy to stay in the air. We took a few pictures at Radstock, struggled on to somewhere between Chilcompton and Binegar, and gave up. Into the wind to Bristol, in heavy traffic, then home on the train. Regret and a sense of failure were tinged with smugness – a difficult decision had been taken with maturity and responsibility... And it really was *very* wet.

In the Summer timetable of 1965 there was no booked steam on timetabled passenger workings through Burton, even on a Saturday. One 'Black Five' reached Derby on a Saturday afternoon, on the 13.40 from Llandudno – I cycled the 10 miles (each way) to Marchington three times to photograph it. Once the weather was poor, once the train was very late and the

Above With the Cotswold scarp behind, 'Britannia' No 70053 *Moray Firth* works upgrade near Winchcombe with the 08.00 Wolverhampton-Ilfracombe train on 10 July 1965. The sky speaks of rain to come... *RNI*

Left As described in the text, there were strange goings-on at Stroud Station on Sunday 11 July 1965 – an LMS 4F has invaded Great Western territory with a breakdown train. The GW 'Manor' beside it looks less out of place but, like the 4F, it is going the wrong way! *MES*

Left It looks like we felt: very wet, in poor condition, and making a big mistake. No 7811 *Dunley Manor* makes its way down the up line through Stroud on the same day. *MES*

Above A rather glum scene at Radstock North: was this what we'd slogged all the way to the S&D for? An LMS 'Jinty' approaches past an LSWR-style signal on 12 July 1965. (If the sign on the left was a trespass notice, it was in a very odd place!) *RNI*

Below Next door we are in a different world, and one even more depressing: this is Radstock West, long closed to passengers, on the same day, with a '5700' Pannier tank and a representative collection of Great Western artefacts. *MES*

Above For the one of us still at school, 28 June 1965 should have been a revision day, but how much better to be at Marchington, on the North Staffs Derby-Crewe line, admiring one of the four named 'Black Fives', No 45156 *Ayrshire Yeomanry*, on an eastbound freight. The military equipment may have been on its way to the nearby depot, though the rail connection was removed the following month. *RNI*

Right Was the white paint the most the shed staff at Oxford had time for? The external condition of No 6991 *Acton Burnell Hall* on 31 July 1965 is typical of GW locos at that time, and it would be withdrawn at the end of the year, but a sound effort is being made on the climb past Hatton North Junction with the 11.38 Poole-Wolverhampton. *RNI*

Below right Same day, same summer sky: No 7804 *Bayford Manor* attacks Hatton Bank with a fitted freight from Basingstoke. *RNI*

light had gone, and once – with a clean engine, a crisp exhaust, and beautiful sunshine – I had forgotten to wind on! As some compensation, on yet another visit to that scenic location we secured a rare shot of a named 'Black Five'.

Not so near, but not too far away, and still very steamy on Summer Saturdays in 1965, was the Snow Hill line. Alas, the Oxley 'Castles' had all gone. Richard had captured a few the year before, and so had I, but what I'm sure would have been my master shots at Knowle & Dorridge, including one of my idol *Sir Edward Elgar*, fell victim to an accident involving Richard's developing tank... (Richard has no memory of this – very Freudian.) But there was still a fair bit of GW power, and Hatton Bank was the obvious destination. Despite the Bath fiasco we planned to go by bike. But our parents took pity on us and subsidised the train fare, about 15 shillings each.

We had the luck to meet up with Wev, more correctly Mr Etherington. He was famous as the doyen of the Moor Street Bridge crowd, and claimed that a postcard addressed to 'Wev, Woodville, S Derbys' had been correctly delivered. His Reliant car was equally famous; crammed in the back together with other acquaintances, we were ferried from one good location between Lapworth and Hatton to another. Before the coming of the motorways, rural Warwickshire was still much as 'BB' had depicted it in his classic children's story *The Little Grey Men* (one of my father's favourite books), and the picture of a 9F and a 'Britannia' meeting north of the Hatton triangle, with the hay just cut, sums it up. On the way home Saltley shed was rich in steam and bathed in sunshine, inviting shots from the train that now have a distinctly valedictory feel.

Above Hay-time: 9F No 92224, coasting down towards Hatton on southbound vans, meets 'Britannia' No 70053 *Moray Firth* on the 10.05 Kingswear-Wolverhampton on 31 July 1965. We probably cursed the impressively well-used telegraph poles for being on the side that was right for the sun, but how they add to the scene! *MES*

Below In this view of Saltley shed yard from the Birmingham-Burton line, local 'Black Five' No 44945, an 8F, a Standard Class 4 and others soak up the evening sun, also on 31 July 1965. *MES*

7

FURTHER AFIELD AGAIN

MIKE: As the rage to take numbers subsided, so also, somehow, did the urge to record every class on film. From late 1963, trips to remoter parts were for action shots. Steam was declining fast, but there were still too many choices. Threatened branch lines? Express steam? Scenic locations? Or just plenty to see? We tried hard, within the financial constraints, to do them all.

28 December 1963 was a nasty dull cold day, but we set out hopefully for Nottingham Victoria and the condemned branch from Nottingham Midland to Worksop (the latter now resuscitated and proudly advertised as the Robin Hood Line). I don't think either of us

had been to Victoria before, so we didn't know what a great big gloomy cave of a place it was, even on a bright day, let alone this dark one. Most of our pictures there are impossibly under-exposed, but in one or two the subject can be made out, and the atmosphere is certainly authentic. For our destination on the Worksop branch we chose Newstead, mainly because it was near Annesley shed. We failed

Nottingham Victoria, 28 December 1963: 'O4' No 63873 stands on the left, while 'Patriot' No 45529 *Stephenson* leaves with what may be the long-running Banbury-York parcels. As a rebuild its power classification was the same as that of a 'Royal Scot'; as an Annesley engine its condition was also the same (see page 72). *MES*

Left 'They can't get the wood, you know...' – remember the Goons? The 'vintage' coach, an early LMS vehicle of 1923-30, looks to have had its wooden body patched with steel, probably owing to a shortage of exotic hardwoods during and after the Second World War. Stanier 2-6-4T No 42628 waits to leave Newstead with a Worksop train on 28 December 1963. *MES*

Below 'K3' 2-6-0s Nos 61907 and 61944 await the attention of scrapman Mr Albert Looms at Spondon in January 1964. According to the *Railway Observer* for that month, No 61907 had towed its sibling to the site from Colwick on 13 November, more than a year after their withdrawal in September 1962. *RNI*

to gain admission there, and the weather was still damp and misty, but the station was out in the open and the shots surprisingly good. From the DMU between Nottingham and Derby we noticed some withdrawn 'K3s', standing forlornly beside the line at Spondon, and we made a brief return the following week to photograph them. They, or their fellows, had looked better on 'The Colwick' (see Chapter 5).

Gloucester was said to be one of the steamiest places left within reach. We heard that it still showed a good variety of GWR types, and that the line from there to Hereford was highly scenic. A return to Gloucester by train was too expensive, so on 25 January 1964 we set off in the dark on the 7.10am Midland Red bus to Birmingham (just under two hours), and thence to Gloucester (almost another three). There was plenty to talk about and look at, so the journey didn't seem over-long. Tewkesbury was a magic name for me because of John Moore's Elmbury books, beloved of my father like those of 'BB'. It was disappointing from the bus route (a visit to the Abbey years later put that right), but Upton-on-Severn looked unspoilt and old-fashioned, with children playing by the river near the town centre.

We got to Gloucester in time to catch the 12.25 to Hereford, with 'Large Prairie' No 4107. Report had not exaggerated the appeal of this wonderful line. The stations were seedy but dignified: can the traffic ever have justified the massive Grange Court? Did a local dignitary demand it? The clank of the tank's motion echoed from the empty platforms. We'd have needed a zoom lens to do justice to Mitcheldean Road, with intimate scenery close by but hints of a larger scale beyond, so we went on to Ross, with its privately run Refreshment Room, then back to Longhope, whence we walked the line to Blaisdon Halt. Ageing GW 'Moguls' and their blockish Hawksworth stock provided some atmospheric shots as the day drew in.

We found plenty to see when we got back to Gloucester, and we planned a return visit for the 'Chalford Auto'. There was heavy rain on 4 April, and our knowledge of the area was inadequate, so the pictures there were disappointing, but we salvaged the day with shots around Central. In the autumn, I would go to the Hereford line again. September was too hot, and without a yellow filter (****!!) the record scarcely matched the reality, but it is enough to spark the memories.

No doubt about it, Gloucester-Hereford took the prize. 'Large Prairie' No 4161 coasts down towards Blaisdon Halt and Gloucester on 12 September 1964. Richard's home printing gives the scene the timeless feel of an early postcard. *MES*

Left Dirty young man? Certainly the mac – we all wore them in those days – would have been after a day on the Gloucester-Hereford line. 'Large Prairie' No 4107 waits to leave Grange Court for Hereford on 25 January 1964. 'Come on, Inwood – you'll miss it!' *RNI*

Below The trim station at Ross-on-Wye, with No 4107 later in its journey. References to services on the Forest of Dean and Wye Valley lines, long since withdrawn, have been expunged from the station sign. *MES*

Left 'Gaunt strong engines' – so Paul Jennings described steam locomotives. GW 'Mogul' No 6349 leaves Blaisdon Halt with a Hereford train on 25 January 1964. *MES*

Return to Gloucester, 4 April 1964: our hopes of emulating George Heiron and Ben Ashworth with idyllic shots of the Golden Valley were dashed by the weather, but at least there was plenty of GW steam. '14XX' 0-4-2T

No 1455 leaves Brimscombe with a down Chalford auto-train (*above*), and with clouds of smoke against a cloudy sky 2-8-0 No 3861 climbs Sapperton Bank with a heavy freight. *Both RNI*

A GW 2-8-0 in different mood on the same day: No 2836 drifts through Gloucester Central with coal from South Wales. In the second view the railway clearly belongs to a different era from its neighbour – perhaps that is the secret of its appeal. The little lad has evidently caught the bug. GW 'Mogul' No 6346 is ready to leave Gloucester Central with the 5.55pm to Hereford. *MES/RNI*

The end of the line in both senses: passenger services between Gloucester and Hereford ceased from 2 November 1964, the same day as the Chalford 'auto'. Visits to the line in the last months still yielded a fine variety of power, not only 'Large Prairies' and a GW 'Mogul', but also a 'Manor', a Pannier tank, a Standard Class 4 4-6-0, and this gem of a Collett 0-6-0 No 2242, seen at Hereford with the 4.30pm to Gloucester on 10 October. *MES*

My final attempt before closure in October started from the Hereford end (on from Birmingham after a music lesson, again by Midland Red), and was rewarded by the motive power on offer (see above). A curiously persistent memory is of a station seat on this line at Ballingham. Incised on it were the words I HAVE SHAGGED JANE TURNER (name changed to spare blushes). Was this an item of information, a triumphant exclamation at the moment of achievement, wishful thinking, or revenge for rejection?

I returned thirty-five years later; the station platform was still there, but alas not the seat. Later still I acquired the Ian Allan *Trains Annual* for 1967, and there on page 93 was a photograph by D. H. Cape (illustrating an article by O. Humberstone Prosser) showing Ballingham station on 24 July 1964, with 'Large Prairie' No 4161 and the identical seat! 'Where are you now, Jane Turner?' as Wilfred

Pickles would have said; who was your lover, and where is he? And what happened to the historic item of furniture that (presumably) witnessed the deed?

Money was still short. Unsporty though we were, we sneaked aboard the school cross-country team's coach to Manchester one Saturday in March, sneaking off again at Buxton and continuing by bus to Peak Forest, to record steam working over the famous Midland Railway summit. The weather was dismal, with continuous drizzle, and the pictures no better – not really good enough to publish, in fact. I suppose it served us right!

RICHARD: Around this time I accepted invitations from fortunate car-owners for trips to Hatton Bank and the Cambrian section. Alas, the weather for the latter was mostly grey, and my memories are grey to match: water dripping from vegetation, and dank periods of waiting around for the trains to come, though the pictures prove that it cleared up later on the second day. Dr Johnson once famously remarked that the Giant's Causeway was worth seeing, but not worth *going* to see. The Cambrian trains and the photographs of them were definitely worth seeing, but I had considerable sympathy with Dr Johnson's point of view...

Closer at hand, but still difficult of access without a car, was that memorable piece of nineteenth-century engineering, the Cromford & High Peak Railway. I made two visits for photography. The first, on 27 June 1964, was for the RCTS special described in Chapter 2, and was accomplished in Bill Pegg's comfortable Austin Cambridge, with Colin Moore, Cliff Shepherd and Phil Waterfield making up a full complement (thanks, Bill, for being so accommodating).

The second trip, on 16 July 1965, was with Mike, Andrew Dow and Iain Wallace. By then the Middleton incline had been taken out, but there was still plenty to see and photograph. Now, at 63, as my wife, Liz, and I walk the so-called High Peak Trail on the trackbed of the line, I try to recall my 19-year-old self chasing round the area by car. Some things are crystal clear, like a glimpse of the workings of the winding house at Sheep Pasture, the wheel itself, and the thickness of the cable. But others are lost in a forty-year-thick mist. What about those footplate shots between Sheep Pasture and Middleton Bottom? Was the loco moving? (Yes it was – there's another shot taken a few hundred yards further on, from the other side of the cab.) But on this (very rare) occasion my memory is better than Mike's, who can't remember the trip at all, but has the pictures to prove he was there!

By the summer of 1964 the remaining GW 'Moguls' were mostly concentrated at Gloucester and Taunton – to see one on an express elsewhere was a rare treat. An unidentified member of the class climbs to Talerddig with the 12.35pm from Aberystwyth to Birmingham Snow Hill on 25 July 1964. *RNI*

Above The peaceful terminus of the Llanfyllin branch, soon to become more peaceful still. 'Mickey Mouse' 2-6-0 No 46512 does the honours on 8 August 1964, with less than six months of the passenger service to run. *RNI*

Below An up express, probably the combined 10.55am Pwllheli-Birmingham and 12.48pm Aberystwyth-Whitchurch, nears Talerddig on 8 August 1964 behind Standard '4' No 75004 and a 'Manor'. *RNI*

Left 0F 0-4-0ST No 47006 heads out from Sheep Pasture towards Black Rocks on the Cromford & High Peak Railway on 16 July 1965. A photograph from the footplate was an added bonus to the day. The shiny new small Nissen hut on the left is still visible today at this location (covered now in moss, etc), but the view of Black Rocks has entirely disappeared due to the growth of the woodland. *RNI*

Below On the same day No 47006 returns with just two wagons. By this date, the 1 in 8 Middleton incline was no longer in operation, so there was limited traffic along this remaining section from the top of the Sheep Pasture incline. *RNI*

MIKE: We knew the writing was on the wall for steam on many routes around the country, and we crammed in as many as we could; if a special visit wasn't possible, a trip ostensibly for other purposes was subtly modified to include a steam line. The next sequence of pictures in this chapter tells that story.

Right On 7 March 1964 Richard and a friend caught a football special from Burton to Manchester, pulled over Peak Forest by a 'Black Five'. They didn't attend the match, whatever it was; instead they continued with steam to Warrington behind Stanier 2-6-4T No 42601, framed here by the famous arched roof at Manchester Central. *RNI*

Below 2-6-4 tanks pass on the CLC route out of Manchester on the same day, giving a fine impression of a busy suburban steam service. *RNI*

Left 'Merchant Navy' 'Pacific' No 35025 *Brocklebank Line* with a down train on the LSWR main line at Sidmouth Junction on 23 May 1964. The weather suits the West of England and somehow adds to the ordinary, even archetypal, nature of the scene. How *permanent* it looks! No such thing, alas – this was already the Western Region, and plans were already afoot to downgrade this former Southern competitor to a secondary route. *MES*

Below Also under Western eyes, and also on the way out, was the S&D branch from Evercreech Junction to Highbridge. '2251' 0-6-0 No 2217 approaches Evercreech on 20 May 1964. The steam in the distance right of centre comes from a more authentic 0-6-0, LMS No 44422 (since preserved), on the S&D main line to Bath. *MES*

Above Blackthorn time: the railway provides a haven for wildlife as Standard Class 5 No 73051 heads away from Blandford Forum on 20 April 1965. Few photographers visited this, the Dorset end of the Somerset & Dorset, and less than a year later the line had closed. *MES*

Below More Western infiltration (in this case, to be fair, a long-established example): No 7808 *Cookham Manor* runs beneath the North Downs scarp, west of Dorking Town, with a Redhill-Reading train on 31 July 1964. *MES*

Left and below left That's better! Indigenous power in the shape of SR 'N' 2-6-0 No 31405 makes a smart getaway from Chilworth & Albury with a Reading-Redhill train on the same day. A visit to this scenic line was made possible by a cunning extension of Mike's annual week of string quartet playing in Berkshire... *MES*

Below Richard's kind offer to drive a neighbour to Manchester (in the gentleman's own car) had a hidden agenda: to see remnants of passenger steam on the Midland route out of Manchester. On 15 July 1965, with a 'Black Five' heading an up train near Buxworth, it looked every bit the through line to London that it was. Now, with the 'Route through the Peak' long gone, there are only two tracks here, and even on the map, let alone the ground, the wide cutting looks empty and forlorn. *MES*

Above A free morning after a conference in Liverpool gave Richard an opportunity to visit the rarely photographed Liverpool-Preston line. Standard Class 4 4-6-0 No 75033 approaches Ormskirk from the Liverpool direction on 19 July 1965. *RNI*

Right and below right One of the last four surviving LNWR locos on BR, 0-8-0 No 49361, is on the 9.30am goods from Water Orton on 13 August 1964. This must have been one of the most famous freights in Britain. It followed the Midland Railway route through Sutton Park and Heath Town to Wolverhampton – or it least it had until a few days before these photographs were taken. From 10 August part of the route was closed to accommodate the Black Country section of the M6 – evidently rail traffic did not warrant a bridge. The train then pursued a circuitous route with several reversals, eventually reaching the far end of the branch via the LNW line through Walsall (hear that ironic snort from 49361?). It is seen here at its ultimate destination, Willenhall (Stafford Street), first by the signal box, then at the long-closed station. *Both RNI*

For the big event of 1964, comparable with the Great Shed Bash of the year before, we went West. First we travelled to Ilfracombe with my parents, who had decided on a holiday there. Poor things, instead of being allowed to go direct from Burton to Taunton and change there, they had to cross Birmingham so we could have steam on the 8.00am train from Wolverhampton to Minehead and Ilfracombe via the North Warwickshire line, diagrammed for an Oxley 'Castle' and duly producing No 7011 *Banbury Castle*. We had hoped for a fast run (as scheduled) from Stratford to Cheltenham, but the crew sensibly took it easy there and made the time up on the less demanding stretch onwards to Bristol, reached 5 minutes early. We had to put up with a 'Hymek' from there to Taunton, but what joy to see plumes of steam above the MPD and a GW 'Mogul' backing on to the Ilfracombe portion. The journey across Somerset and North Devon on that steeply graded, highly scenic and often remote single line (poignantly celebrated in David St John Thomas's *The Country Railway*, and now no more) was a highlight of the year.

The GW 'Moguls' and the LMS Ivatt 2-6-2 tanks dominated the week to come. Barnstaple-Taunton was disappointing; the scenic spots were hard to get to. Why didn't we take more station shots? Our late lamented colleague Biffo used to say 'I like life in my pictures – plant life', and that's how we thought, but it's yet another source of regret. For Torrington to Halwill we had little choice – a straight return trip was the only possibility – but the schedule allowed plenty of time at stations, so station shots was what we got. And – how ungrateful can you get? – without a yellow filter (again) the weather was *too good*: very bright and very hot, except in the early morning.

At the end of the week, my parents went home (via the sensible route), while we travelled to Bristol via Exeter, Templecombe and the S&D. An 'N' to Exeter, an unrebuilt 'Pacific' to Templecombe, an LMS tank to Evercreech and a Standard Class 5 to Bath. Too bright again, but we got some nice S&D shots, including the last working S&D 2-8-0 on Templecombe shed. From Bristol to Swansea on a Sunday was not exactly steamy. However, we paid the obligatory visit to Mr Woodham at Barry, and got quite a long way round the scrap line before the police ejected us.

From that Welsh Sunday, it is non-railway details that stick in the mind: a Methodist church service in Swansea, and a hymn that neither of us knew, 'Lord Jesus, bless us ere we go', but that has remained with us ever since, and the infestation of curious insects, like small red-brown cockroaches, in the washroom of the Swansea YMCA. (They were there in 1962, as well. What were they? Are they still there now? Or have they gone the way of Jane Turner's bench?)

Carmarthen-Aberystwyth gave us a BR '80XXX' tank rather than the hoped-for 'Manor', but it could have been a 'Hymek', and how lucky we are to have travelled that soon-to-be-closed link in the most westerly through route from South to North Wales (we completed it later in the week with another doomed section, from Afon Wen to Bangor).

In central Wales we met up with our friends Cliff and Roger, and between the four of us, based at Machynlleth and Harlech, we managed a fair coverage: Welshpool, Oswestry, Talerddig (weather too good again; beautiful hills, rural quiet, barn owl in the cutting, wood-wasp slain by Roger's lemonade bottle), Aberdovey, Morfa Mawddach, Barmouth, Pwllheli, the Amlwch branch, Menai Bridge, Bangor, Chester. The greatest reward on the North Wales Coast was the working remnant of 'Royal Scots' and rebuilt 'Patriots'.

On the last day three of us opted for the Barmouth-Ruabon line and the Bala branch. Roger, cunningly, went back to the coast, in the hope of photographing a 'Coronation'. This he did (it was No 46238 *City of Carlisle*), and he spent some time on the footplate at Rhyl, but he is still kicking himself for failing to secure a ride. If only his strategy had been slightly different! We all met up at Shrewsbury, with no money to get home. Roger's kind Dad came all the way from Burton to fetch us. Perhaps things have changed less than we like to think: parents were chauffeurs even then...

Right Another rare express turn for a GW 'Mogul' (see page 86): No 6326 climbs through Milverton with the Ilfracombe portion of the 8.00am train from Wolverhampton to Minehead and Ilfracombe on 15 August 1964, the first day of our Devon holiday. *MES*

Below 'Sun destroys / The interest of what's happening in the shade': Philip Larkin's words were evoked by the 'long cool platforms' of stations on the East Coast Main Line, seen from the train on a hot Whit Saturday. They apply equally to this view of Barnstaple Junction on Saturday 22 August 1964. No 6326 must have been flavour of the month at Taunton shed, for here it is again with Class 'A' headlamps on the opposite number of the train in the previous picture. *RNI*

Above A Barnstaple-Taunton train with a GW 'Mogul' crosses one of the line's distinctive viaducts, Castle Hill near Filleigh, on 20 August 1964. This is *Tarka the Otter* country; our walk to the photo-spot took us past Henry Williamson's house at Shallowford. *MES*

Left At Torrington on the same day, LMS 2-6-2Ts Nos 41208 and 41223 have rapidly and memorably double-headed our early-morning train from Barnstaple. No 41208 has uncoupled and will work to Halwill. *MES*

Left The Torrington-Halwill branch proved the truth of the dictum that the later a line was built, the less successful it was. As David St John Thomas says, 'Barely one passenger a week used Hatherleigh's well-kept station,' seen here on 22 August 1964. 'It was as if Waterloo had forgotten the line, or it was deemed indecent to close a railway opened as recently as 1925.' With Paddington in charge, however, closure took place on 1 March 1965. *RNI*

Above S&D 2-8-0 No 53807 is still working at Templecombe on 22 August 1964. In the background are two interloping '2251s'. *MES*

Right The following day we discovered the next member of the class, No 53808, amidst the undergrowth on the famous Barry scrapline. Two years before we had seen it in steam at Bath (see page 13). Thanks to Mr Woodham it survived into preservation. *RNI*

Right The Barry graveyard, with GWR and SR 4-6-0s, on 23 August 1964. *RNI*

Above Standard Class 4 4-6-0 No 75002 runs up the coast near Aberdovey on 26 August 1964. *RNI*

Below Standard Class 3 2-6-2T No 82034 leaves Morfa Mawddach for Barmouth on the same day, with Cader Idris in the background. *RNI*

Above You might find such a barrow-load on a preserved line today, but this was for real. Whence and whither the barrel? 2-6-2T No 41226 blows off at Llangefni, on the Amlwch branch on Anglesey, on 28 August 1964. *RNI*

Below Driver (thinks): 'Cranks, parasites – catch me posing for them…' Fireman: 'You wouldn't be so keen on steam if you had to fire the bloody things, not that you could.' Or were we being paranoid? 'Royal Scot' No 46152 *The King's Dragoon Guardsman* again (see page 6), this time at Bangor on 27 August 1964, complete with yellow stripe. *MES*

Mike's favourite shot: Standard Class 4 2-6-4 tank No 80105 leaves Barmouth with a morning train to Paddington on 29 August 1964. *MES*

8
THE USES OF EDUCATION

MIKE: From 1958 to 1965 I was lucky enough to receive a grant for music lessons with the great Birmingham teacher Christopher Edmunds, a pupil of Granville Bantock, at his house in Solihull. From Birmingham to Solihull and back the journey was usually by bus, but between Burton and Birmingham I used the train. My mother, who chaperoned me for the first couple of years, always insisted that I was more interested in the trains than the music, and there was an element of truth in this, though the lessons were always enjoyable and worthwhile. The outward journey was by local DMU, but the return was on the 10.30am Bristol-Newcastle (12.47 from Birmingham), sharply timed, heavily loaded, almost invariably late, and up to June 1961 usually 'Jubilee'-hauled. I would give a lot for some shots of it entering New Street or leaving Burton before the diesels came.

Even in later years, though, there was plenty to see, and increasingly often the 12.47 was allowed to go and the afternoon spent watching and photographing trains. This was most frequently at Snow Hill, but there were also visits to Tyseley, Bentley Heath, West Bromwich, Brickyard Crossing on the Camp Hill line, and King's Norton. Birmingham was used as a jumping-off point for Bromyard, Hereford (see Chapter 7) and Shrewsbury; on such occasions, to save money, the whole of the day's travel might be by Midland Red bus, with a Day Anywhere ticket, leaving Burton around 7.00am and getting back just before midnight.

The last day of the Burton-Wolverhampton (DMU) passenger service was marked by a train journey via Walsall, with a visit to Bescot on the return. A sad day: cold and wet, with a row of withdrawn LNW 0-8-0s ('Duck 8s' as we called them) at Bescot (where more recently similar lines of condemned diesels could be found); No 92220 *Evening Star*, filthy, on a freight; chilly Danish Blue sandwiches on the gloomy old Walsall station (better than the lavatorial new one, though – and surely they could have saved the wonderful entrance hall?); and the demise of the trains by which we used to go, as young spotters, to Lichfield Trent Valley or to Wolverhampton itself.

My last session with Chris (or Dr Edmunds, as he was then known) was on 3 July 1965. Exceptionally, this was an afternoon visit, and it was not a lesson but a farewell, with my mother present and also Arthur Ormerod, the former Headmaster of my junior school, who had fostered my musical interests and had secured the grant for study with Chris. It was a moving occasion, and something of a milestone, but of course the most had to be made of it in railway terms, so I set off first and took a trip from Snow Hill to Leamington and back. No 6803 *Bucklebury Grange* (which, so former Stourbridge Junction fireman David Holloway said recently, 'would steam on nothing') made a lively outward run on the 11.10 Wolverhampton-Weymouth, and No 6976 *Graythwaite Hall* coped manfully on the 09.23 train from Bournemouth to Liverpool and Manchester, beating the (admittedly generous) schedule with twelve packed coaches. It was a good way to end.

Above 'Britannia' No 70033 *Charles Dickens* is on the North Western side of Birmingham New Street, rebuilt without an overall roof after wartime bombing. Soon the whole station will have not an overall roof but an overhead shopping centre and car park – instead of asserting its identity it will apologise for its existence. Under construction in the background is the then ultra-modern Rotunda, now a treasured heritage item. *MES*

Below The Midland side of New Street was not rebuilt after the war, but the totem, the box with the splendid pre-Grouping-pattern signals beyond, the bridge, and the lovingly detailed edifice above will soon be swept away in favour of something like the Brutalist tat in the extreme top right-hand corner. Also left over from a previous age, and soon to go, is Horwich 'Crab' No 42703, an amazing sight on 19 September 1964 with the 6.45am Gloucester-Sheffield express. *MES*

Above Great Western 4-6-0 No 6953 *Leighton Hall* brings an up freight through Tyseley on 6 March 1965. *MES*

Right 'Large Prairie' No 4155 looks neat and efficient as it bustles along the GW main line near Bentley Heath with a down freight on 27 March 1965. *MES*

Below The one that nearly got away: Saltley 'Jubilee' No 45674 *Duncan* was usually kept in good condition for just such a job as this, replacing a failed 'Peak' on the 08.20 Newcastle-Cardiff of 1 February 1964, seen here passing King's Norton. With the steel train in front, the shot could have been abandoned, but the result is much more interesting than a 'standard three-quarter'. Thank you, Mr Gifford! *MES*

Left That it should come to this! British Railways' Last Steam Locomotive, No 92220 *Evening Star*, passes Bescot on 16 January 1965. Remember the fuss when it was built? A competition to name it, a naming ceremony, a commemorative plaque (you can see the scars left by it and the nameplate). If ever a picture told a story of doom and gloom, this is it. The engine is filthy (and a man who worked on it says that alone among the class it was useless anyway!). The electrification masts have gone up, the signal box in the distance will soon be coming down – compare it with the rubbish on the right. *MES*

Below 'Modified Hall' No 6976 *Graythwaite Hall* runs into Leamington with the 09.23 Bournemouth to Liverpool and Manchester on 3 July 1965. *MES*

RICHARD: By the summer of 1965 I had already had one year at Oxford, and had made the most of the time. Usually with Andrew Dow, I had many a quick run out by bike from the centre of the city to Aristotle Lane, Port Meadow, Wolvercote Junction, Hinksey, and Oxford Station itself, to catch the dying gasps of steam, especially on the Bournemouth-York express in each direction, with 'Halls', 'Modified Halls' and Bulleid 'Pacifics'. A University Grant (of blessed memory) made colour film accessible and, without really being aware of recording history, that is, in fact, what we did. Most of my pictures from that first academic year make it look as though it was always sunny in Oxford, but the memory of a disastrous attempt to photograph Winston Churchill's funeral train on 30 January 1965 destroys the illusion. The now famous train ran from Waterloo to bring Churchill to his final resting place at Bladon near Blenheim. We had a raw wait for the train, pulled (predictably enough) by the eponymous unrebuilt Bulleid 'Pacific' No 34051. My diary – written before the photos were developed – contains the hopeful entry, 'Went to Yarnton for picture of Winston Churchill's funeral train (got what might be quite a good one)'. In fact, at the crucial moment the wind blew and the whole of the train apart from the front of the locomotive was rendered invisible.

Excursions behind steam took place as often as possible, to Banbury (as on the front cover), Kingham, and Thame.

However, Oxford shed closed at the end of 1965, and that was the end of the 'Halls'; thereafter 'Black Fives' or Bulleids worked through to and from Banbury, until the end of the Great Central on 3 September 1966 and the diversion of the train via Birmingham. By that time there was precious little left to see, and the Epilogue recounts the waning of interest that accompanied the decline. But it was good while it lasted; for both of us, educational opportunities had been put to good use!

Above Standard 9F 2-10-0 No 92029 (formerly fitted with a Crosti boiler) accelerates north under Oxford's Aristotle Lane bridge with a fitted freight during the winter of 1965. Even now, a boarded crossing also allows allotment holders to cross the line here, though now there are just three tracks, the line on the right joining the Down Fast just at the bridge. *RNI*

Below On a glorious day in the spring of 1965, 'West Country' Class Bulleid 'Pacific' No 34018 *Axminster* gets the southbound York-Bournemouth moving from Oxford Station. The shot is taken from the Olney Lane footbridge. Returning in 2008 (to get a '40-plus years on' photograph) Richard discovered the bridge had been demolished – though there is a promise posted nearby that it will be replaced in due course. *RNI*

Compared with the rather decorous departure of a Bulleid 'Pacific', 'Modified Hall' No 6980 *Llanrumney Hall* makes a more vigorous approach to the same 'coign of vantage', again in the spring of 1965, and hurries on south past the cemetery towards the bridge over the Isis. *Both RNI*

By the time these pictures were taken number and name plates had been recognised as collectors' items. The 'Hall' Class loco here has its number chalked on, making identification precarious – the best guess narrows it down to No 693?. However, it is clearly still capable of working well as it accelerates its train towards Banbury north of Wolvercote Junction, probably on 20 May 1965. *Both RNI*

Left 'Battle of Britain' Class No 34064 *Fighter Command* eases its stock northward between Kennington and South Hinksey on 17 May 1965. *RNI*

Below left If it weren't for this photograph, we might have wondered if we'd had too much refreshment in Banbury Station bar on a hot summer's day. But this *is* a snowplough; this *is* a BR Standard 9F 2-10-0; and it *is* late May or early June 1965. Go figure! *RNI*

Above On 5 June 1965 Andrew Dow and Richard travelled on the ThSO 13.25 Oxford to Kingham 'Market Train' – surely a real Great Western survival. For some inexplicable reason, the stock continued to Worcester empty. 'Hall' Class 4-6-0 No 6947 *Helmingham Hall* waits at Hanborough station, probably for Richard. Andrew can be glimpsed at the rear of the train holding the door open! Clearly visible is a change in platform level: was it engineered for Winston Churchill's funeral train, which terminated here? *RNI*

Right A stop at Ascott-under-Wychwood gave the opportunity to record the fashions of the time as our fellow passengers left the train. *RNI*

9
NO WONDER THEY
THOUGHT WE WERE MAD

MIKE: The nearer the end, the more desperate we got. At Easter 1965 we realised (long after everyone else) that the antique locos and carriages on the Isle of Wight couldn't last much longer (alternatives had already been mooted and closure proposed), so ... once again those useful people, parents, were pressed into service, and Richard's father turned out at 4.00am to take us to Derby. It was a poor reward to have the 'Peak' fail at Luton, and we eventually reached Portsmouth from Waterloo an hour and a half later than planned. Still, there were plenty of ferries, and plenty of trains on the Island. It was a lovely day, and the railway banks around Smallbrook Junction and on the Newport line were covered in primroses and the beautiful pink and blue flowers of the scarce native lungwort *Pulmonaria longifolia*. The IOW was never the best place for lineside views, and the station shots were the best (why didn't we learn?). But we got a feel for the place and the system, and I would return for railways and botany the next year, before the 'O2s' eventually disappeared. We were back at Burton by 1.00am the next day.

We must have got a taste for this sort of thing, because only a week or so later we made another (not quite so) early start, this time for the Somerset & Dorset. And again the 'Peak' failed, and this time the weather wasn't kind, and in fact the trip was a washout, though not such a washout as our later, longer and harder jaunt to the line (see Chapter 6).

But we didn't give up. Steam, and especially steam on passenger, must be followed wherever it went, and by the summer of 1965 that meant

- the Snow Hill line (see Chapter 6)
- the Southern (but we'd done that)
- North Wales (but we'd done that too, and in any case the Cambrian was not what it had been, with Standards replacing 'Manors', and DMUs on the locals)
- the North West.

So we joined the pilgrimage to Carlisle. For 35 shillings you could get a seven-day Rover ticket that took in the Border City, Skipton via Settle, Lancaster via Shap, the coast line, and all points between. That summer we saved up for two of them.

For the first trip, in the genial company of Colin Moore, we'd failed to do our homework properly. We knew that on Fridays 'Jubilee' No 45698 *Mars* had a regular passenger turn over Shap. We'd got it into our half-witted heads that this was the 16.35 Liverpool-Glasgow, so having reached Lancaster (steam-hauled) from Crewe, we took a trip up to Oxenholme, only to meet *Mars* on our return, heading the 13.10 FO. SPONNED, as the Goons used to say! (Yes, of course, we should have guessed.) Still, there was plenty to see at Lancaster, and, when we got there behind an English Electric Type 4, at Carlisle. We tried to get a kip on a station barrow, but it was all too exciting. (In T. S. Eliot's *Old Possum's Book of Practical Cats*, there is a wonderful picture by Nicolas Bentley showing the scene at Citadel Station as

Above The Isle of Wight, 3 April 1965: after a protracted overnight journey, this 'O2' was a sight for bleary eyes as it left Ryde Pier Head with a Cowes train. What was the bell on the pole for? *MES*

Below 'O2' No 30 gets the stage to itself with a train to Ryde. *RNI*

Above No 22 stands at Sandown, with its unusual signal box. *RNI*

Below We weren't called 'anoraks' then, but we could still be an object of derision to the local inhabitants: No 30 and a proper local train (period stock, full of people) from Ryde. *RNI*

Above The time of year is evident from the primroses, and the part of the country from the weather. This is Bath again (see Chapter 6), and on 8 April 1965 Standard Class 4 4-6-0 No 75072 emerges from Devonshire Tunnel, in what was later to be one of Richard's parishes! *RNI*

Below Murphy's Law in operation: the sun comes out just in time for the last shot of the day. Standard Class 3 2-6-2T No 82036 stands at Bath Green Park with a Bristol train on the same day. *RNI*

Mickey Mouse crosses the Lune: an LMS Class 2 2-6-0 north of Lancaster on 23 July 1965. *RNI*

Skimbleshanks the Railway Cat 'greets the station-master with elation'; we felt a bit like that.)

The plan was to travel to Skipton in the early hours, and come back on the night St Pancras-Glasgow relief, the famous 02.25 from Leeds City, diagrammed for a 'Jubilee'. We'd hoped for steam in the up direction too, but the Edinburgh extra, with a 'Black Five', wasn't stopping before Leeds, so we had to put up with a 'Peak'. We waited a long time at Skipton on a dark, deserted platform; 3 o'clock came and went, and at last the pegs came off. Steam! But it wasn't going to stop, and it was an LNER whistle, not an LMS hoot, that drove us back from the platform edge as 'A1' No 60131 *Osprey* swept by with seven near-empty coaches. Another long wait – the 02.25 was very late. Then the pegs came off again, there was the familiar noise of Stanier motion, and round the curve came a Stanier profile.

'It's a little Five,' said Colin.

'No,' I said confidently, 'they go "clonk", this goes "clink". It's a Jubilee.'

'You lucky sod,' said Colin as No 45697 *Achilles* drew to a stand by the water column.

We left well over an hour late. 'A Jubilee at its beautiful best!' yelled Colin as we roared up to Bell Busk. He found the Guard and got the scheduled passing times and the information that the crew were 'as keen as mustard'. We looked for the lighted signal boxes and shouted the times and speeds to each other (poor ordinary passengers – why didn't they lynch us?). The dip at Settle Junction produced 70, then we settled down to a steady 34 up the Long Drag. It sounded wonderful, but even with 73 through Garsdale and 65 at Ais Gill we had lost 2 minutes 17 seconds to this point. We were doing 78 through Mallerstang, and things were looking up, when on came the brakes. A Sulzer Type 2 with a freight had been put out in front of us, and we were checked most of the way to Carlisle. A fine view of mist on the Eden at daybreak was not much compensation.

'We were going, but they wouldn't let us,' said the fireman when we got there (see the picture on page 2).

We'd decided on Garsdale for the day's photography, so it was back again, with a 'Black Five' on the Hellifield slow. We staggered to Garsdale Troughs, and were sorting ourselves out when a harsh purring heralded, as we thought, a 'Peak' on the 10.35 ex-Leeds. But no – it was No 45626 *Seychelles* on the Birmingham CTAC Tours special, which we'd forgotten all about. SPONNED again! But we were better placed for No 45675 *Hardy*

Above 'Black Five' No 45481 has just brought us to Garsdale with the early-morning stopper to Hellifield on 24 July 1965. *RNI*

Below 'Jubilee' No 45675 *Hardy* passes Garsdale Troughs with the 06.40 Birmingham-Glasgow on the same day. *RNI*

Although 'A1' 'Pacifics' worked quite frequently over the Settle & Carlisle in the last years of steam, photographs of them there are rare, so we were pleased to bag No 60131 *Osprey* at Dandry Mire with the Saturday 09.50 Edinburgh (Waverley)-Carlisle on 24 July 1965. *RNI*

on the 06.40 from Birmingham, and the view of Garsdale curving away into a typical Settle & Carlisle haze has never gone away...

Tramping to and fro between the troughs, Dandry Mire Viaduct (beneath which marsh orchids and twayblades grew in a typical Pennine mire habitat) and Moorcock Tunnel exhausted us after our sleepless night. Richard actually fell asleep on the slope above the tunnel. ('He's creased,' said Colin.) But it was worth it for the returning 'A1' and my favourite 'Jubilee', No 45660 *Rooke*. This was one of the famous Bristol Barrow Road stud, and it gave me my fastest time ever with steam from Birmingham to Burton, on the good old 12.47 (see Chapter 8). More famously still, it had done wonders on a test train over Ais Gill in 1937, and it was good to see it back at the scene of its former triumphs – though, alas, it was late and dirty and run-down (later we heard that it had a cracked frame!).

The long journey home included another 'Black Five' on the Bradford stopper (see the title page); fish and chips by the canal in Skipton; a 'Peak' to Leeds; a Type 2 to Sheffield (Richard, asleep again at full length, was swept off the seat by a large and intimidating Yorkshireman); and another 'Peak' on the Newcastle-Bristol mail, with an arrival in Burton at 00.46. Almost before we got home we were making plans to go back; twenty years later my parents were still imitating me saying, 'I must go over Shap again'. They thought we were mad, of course – and no wonder.

Go back we did, for *Mars* over Shap (a good effort, unassisted, with a heavy load), and several other trips over the fells, culminating in double-headed 'Black Fives' on the 21.50 Perth-Euston sleeper (25 minutes gained on schedule between Carlisle and Crewe). The weather was good for photography, which was mainly at the classic site above Oxenholme. But what sticks in the mind from this second effort are the missed opportunities: a 'Clan' over Beattock; the Lakeside branch; above all, the Cockermouth, Keswick & Penrith. At the risk of tediousness – if only!

Above A poignant view on the Settle & Carlisle of an express from St Pancras to Glasgow. Typical S&C weather; the engine that set up record times on the route in 1937; and the kind of picture you could have taken here, featuring the same class of loco, at any time between then and the date of this one. The 09.30 Summer Saturday relief to the 'Thames-Clyde Express' approaches Moorcock Tunnel on 24 July 1965 behind 'Jubilee' No 45660 *Rooke. MES*

Below Oxenholme, summer 1965: LMS 2-6-4 tank No 42080 banks 'Black Five' No 45118 away from the station on the evening of 26 August; the Windermere line diverges to the left. *MES*

Above A 9F sets off from Oxenholme to tackle Grayrigg bank, with a 2-6-4 tank assisting, on 28 August 1965. *RNI*

Below A 2-6-4T blows a nonchalant smoke-ring as it drifts past imperturbable cows after a banking session on the same day. *MES*

EPILOGUE

RICHARD: Although there was still plenty of steam around in 1966, and a fair bit in 1967, we'd done many of the railway things we'd wanted to do, and we didn't give it so much attention. I started going out with Liz in November 1967 (Mike, a slow starter – he says – didn't acquire a girlfriend until 1968). In addition, both of us were becoming more and more involved with other activities, which, in my case, eventually determined the direction of my life, so neither of us joined any railway society at Oxford or Cambridge.

For Mike, meeting one fellow-student of English who was a highly competent botanist, and another who was a knowledgeable birdwatcher, resulted in those earlier interests, latent since the onset of the Railway Bug, being reawakened. For me, my Christian faith came of age in my first term, ceasing simply to be a background part of my life and moving centre stage, a position it had long occupied for fellow enthusiast Andrew Dow, who like me was later ordained.

The unkempt condition of this 'Black Five' (poor successors to 'Halls') was typical of the last months of steam on the York-Bournemouth, seen here passing Wolvercote. *RNI*

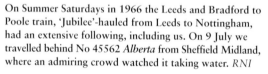

On Summer Saturdays in 1966 the Leeds and Bradford to Poole train, 'Jubilee'-hauled from Leeds to Nottingham, had an extensive following, including us. On 9 July we travelled behind No 45562 *Alberta* from Sheffield Midland, where an admiring crowd watched it taking water. *RNI*

Two weeks later, on 23 July 1966, we opted for the action shot. *Alberta* climbs from Dore & Totley to Bradway Tunnel with the same train. *RNI*

As time went by, moreover, what steam there was became less atractive. 'Black Fives', together with 8Fs, a handful of other LMS types and, of course, the Standard classes, seemed to be dominant almost everywhere, as British Railways sensibly (from its point of view) sought to reduce maintenance costs by reducing the number of designs in service.

The survival of a handful of 'Jubilees' into 1967 is one of the stranger-than-fiction legends of railway lore, and we did pursue them, together with the 'Britannias' (and even the 'Black Fives'), in the North West. I have a strong memory of a bunch of us racing around in the aforementioned Austin Cambridge, risking all to photograph the remaining steam passenger turns on the Settle & Carlisle and

Shap in the same afternoon; and we paid our dues to the railway by taking memorable trips on a number of routes.

We could, of course, have joined the cross-Channel exodus – steam in Europe persisted long after its extinction in the UK. In fact, our only European venture was more or less fortuitous, the result of Mike winning a prize from the Hispanic Council to visit Spain. The finance for my travel came not from any effort or brilliance on my part but from a wonderful benefaction at University College, Oxford, which was for students to travel to visit places *unconnected* with their course of study. As I was a Chemist, a tour of Spain qualified for a grant. My shots of RENFE locos represent a fraction of what we could have had if we'd been more single-minded about railways on that trip...

Above The 13.10 FO Liverpool and Manchester to Glasgow passes a 'Pig' on an up tripper north of Preston. The steam at the front end is from 'Black Five' No 44889, replacing a failed Brush Type 4 on 7 July 1967. *RNI*

Below With eleven full coaches, No 44889 had to pause for assistance at Tebay and Standard Class 4 No 75039 obliged. However, the run was creditable overall, with a top speed of 85mph down the other side. *RNI*

Above 'Black Five' exchange at Carlisle: No 45259 relieves No 44889 on the 13.10 Liverpool and Manchester to Glasgow service on 7 July 1967. *RNI*

Below You had to go there sometime (and soon it would be too late): 'Britannia' No 70016 *Ariel* crosses Ribblehead Viaduct with the 09.20 St Pancras-Glasgow on 22 July 1967, disappointing those who were expecting a 'Jubilee'. *RNI*

Above You had to go there too: 'Black Five' No 44876 climbs past Shap Wells with the 11.55 Euston-Carlisle on the same day. The loco and train in this picture and the previous one were identified from Derek Huntriss's excellent *London Midland in the Fells*. Evidently Mr Huntriss, like Richard's driver, did a Graham Hill (remember him?) over the Pennines that afternoon. *RNI*

Below The end of the day is nearing in more ways than one as the westering sun catches 'Britannia' No 70038 *Robin Hood* on the descent from Shap Summit with the 14.00 train from Glasgow to Liverpool and Manchester on 22 July 1967. *RNI*

Above The twin single-line bores of Standedge Tunnel closed on 30 October 1966. They were obviously still in use on 23 July when we passed behind Standard Class 5 No 73006, about to enter the double-line portal with the Saturday 11.25 Newcastle-Llandudno. *RNI*

Below 'A4' 'Pacific' No 60024 *Kingfisher* looks rather lost at Wetmore Sidings, Burton, as it heads for home in Scotland after working an enthusiasts' special on the Southern Region in March 1966. *MES*

And what of Burton? Steam actually persisted longer there than in many other places, though sightings became sparse after the shed closed to steam on 9 September 1966; but Mike had said a ritual farewell before departing for Cambridge in October 1965, and we were rarely at the lineside to witness the decline. I have no Burton pictures at all after 1965, and Mike can find only half a dozen. His rare shot of an 'A4' at Wetmore Sidings must have been the result of a tip-off; it looks completely incongruous, and nobody could have foretold the later visits by other members of the class in the preservation era. Certainly unplanned, however, was a sequence showing a 'Jinty' on the Horninglow branch on 13 April 1966; the regular engine had been a diesel for nearly a year. Mike managed a footplate ride as well – altogether a nice present on his nineteenth birthday.

The late harvest, then, was rather meagre. With hindsight, we should have been chasing 'Q6s' and 'J27s' in the North East (Mike was actually there in August 1967, but either wasn't aware or couldn't be bothered) and run-down 'B1s' in Yorkshire (an after-dark run from Doncaster to Sheffield at Easter 1966 might have pointed the way); attending the last rites on the Great Central (even with 'Black Fives'); recording the last 'Jinties' at Williamthorpe Colliery.

But nostalgia's not what it used to be, so enough of 'if only'. We're grateful for what we saw, and for what we've got.

Down your street: 'Jinty' No 47643 shunts across Victoria Crescent, Burton, where Mike was brought up, with the Horninglow branch trip on 13 April 1966. *MES*

ACKNOWLEDGEMENTS

We have dedicated this book in gratitude to our parents, Eric and Jessica Smith and Cib and Sylvia Inwood. One or other of them accompanied our early wanderings, patiently delivered us to 4.00am departures and put up with detours on car or rail journeys to catch some vital steam event. It's what parents do! Wonderfully, Jessica is still with us, and is able to enjoy our nostalgia.

As the milestone of forty years of marriage to Liz approaches, Richard wants to thank her for those years – and also for embracing the revival of this long-dormant part of his life.

A chance re-acquaintance with Sheila, the wife of David St John Thomas, led to him kindly agreeing to write a Foreword for us. We are very grateful to this distinguished railway author and publisher for endorsing our efforts in this way.

We owe a huge debt to Mike Thompson, who not only fostered our interest but also entrusted us with the running of the Club he founded. A number of friends who shared our railway odyssey have been helpful in confirming locations and dates. We are particularly grateful to Roger Newman, Andrew Dow and Cliff Shepherd, author of the meticulously researched *Brewery Railways of Burton on Trent*. Andrew also introduced Richard, long ago, to Robert Wade, whose head graces the front cover! Hugh McQuade, of the Severn Valley Railway, supplied fascinating information about coaching stock. Of course, any remaining errors are entirely our responsibility.

At the start of our work together, Mr and Mrs J. L. Forrester of Halesowen Photo Centre were very helpful in producing (from a huge number of negatives) the initial 750 prints from which we made our final selection.

Will Adams and his colleagues at Silver Link Publishing have been enthusiastic, helpful and very accommodating of our wishes. It's been great working with them and, again, we are very grateful.

Confession time

A word about the photographs. In almost every case, they have only been cropped and/or retouched to remove scratches and blemishes. However, we want to be entirely honest about the four that have had a little invasive surgery.

Opposite the title page there is a photograph taken in the very early morning. In its original form, the vertical alignment reflected both excitement and lack of sleep. This has now been rectified with a little judicious 'cloning' at the top left.

On page 23 a photograph features an 'Austerity' about to pass Burton South box. Mike's hand and camera were unhappy additions to the left of Richard's shot, so some signal box boarding has been 'cloned' to replace them.

On page 37 there is a photograph of two 'J94s' at Prestwich Intake crossing. The picture was taken from a car, and the car's mirror has been 'removed'.

In the final shot of the Epilogue ('Jinty' No 47643) Mike left the poor railwayman with no feet. We have given him some!

Otherwise, what you see is what we saw!

ABBREVIATIONS

BR	British Railways
BTC	British Transport Commission
C&HPR	Cromford & High Peak Railway
CLC	Cheshire Lines Committee
CTAC	Creative Tourist Agents' Conference
DMU	Diesel Multiple Unit
GC(R)	Great Central (Railway)
GN(R)	Great Northern (Railway)
GW(R)	Great Western (Railway)
LB&SCR	London Brighton & South Coast Railway
LMS	London Midland & Scottish [Railway]
LNE(R)	London & North Eastern (Railway)
LNW(R)	London & North Western (Railway)
LSW(R)	London & South Western (Railway)
MPD	Motive Power Depot
MR	Midland Railway

RCTS	Railway Correspondence & Travel Society
S&C	Settle & Carlisle
S&D(JR)	Somerset & Dorset (Joint Railway)
SLS	Stephenson Locomotive Society
SR	Southern Railway
TPO	Travelling Post Office
WCML	West Coast Main Line
WRC	"Wanderers" Railfans' Club
ThSO	Thursdays and Saturdays only
FO	Fridays only
SO	Saturdays only

Below 'Jubilee' No 45720 *Indomitable*, minus nameplates, awaiting scrap at Lugton Dump, north of Kilmarnock, on 24 August 1963. *MES*

Inset Fortunately, at least one of *Indomitable*'s nameplates was saved. *RNI*

INDEX OF PHOTOGRAPHIC LOCATIONS